30119 022 175 170

WA

D0537260

This book is to be returned on or before the last date stamped below.

1 8 FEB 2003		

LEARNING FOR LIFE
LONDON BOROUGH OF SUTTON LIBRARIES

WALLINGTON LIBRARY
SHOT
WAL   W6 0HY
TEL   00

RENEWALS   Please quote: date of return, your ticket number
and computer label number for each item.

interiors

gardens

simply

zen

consultant
editor

d a v i d
s c o t t

new holland

contents

This edition first published in 2002 by
New Holland Publishers (UK) Ltd
London • Cape Town • Sydney • Auckland

Garfield House, 86-88 Edgware Road
London W2 2EA
United Kingdom

80 McKenzie Street
Cape Town 8001
South Africa

Level 1, Unit 4, 14 Aquatic Drive
Frenchs Forest, NSW 2086
Australia

218 Lake Road
Northcote, Auckland
New Zealand

Copyright © 1999 in text David Scott,
Siân Evans, Marc Peter Keane
Copyright © 1999 New Holland
Publishers (UK) Ltd

All rights reserved. No part of this
publication may be reproduced, stored in
a retrieval system, or transmitted in any
form or by any means, electronic, mechan-
ical, photocopying, recording or otherwise,
without the prior written permission of the
publishers and copyright holders.

ISBN 1 84330 338 8 (pb)

Introduction written by David Scott
Zen Interiors text written by Siân Evans
Zen Gardens text by written by
Marc Peter Keane

Mark Peter Keane's garden designs appear
on pages 90, 110, 114, 115, 117 and 118.

Designer: Grahame Dudley
Picture Researcher: Christine Rista
Editorial Assistant: Anke Ueberberg

Editorial Direction: Yvonne McFarlane

10 9 8 7 6 5 4 3 2 1

Reproduction by PICA Colour Separation,
Singapore
Printed and bound in Singapore

LONDON BOROUGH
LIBRARY SERVICE
022175170
NOV 2002

747

Gardens 86

by Marc Peter Keane

below: A weather-worn stone sculpture of Siddhartha Gautama, founder of Buddhism, upon which Zen is based, with two senior followers. Zen respects the transformation of natural materials through ageing, as seen in this stone figure.

Introduction

by David Scott

The philosophy of Zen Buddhism and the values associated with it – simplicity, restraint and naturalness – together with other aspects of Japanese culture and geography, have had an important influence on the development of traditional Japanese gardens and architecture. In *Simply Zen*, we explore their design, construction and Zen aesthetic and explain how its ideas and spiritual values can be applied in a practical manner, whether on a large or small scale, to our own living spaces. By introducing Zen ideals of tranquillity and repose and the appreciation of Nature into western homes we may, perhaps, bring to our lives a sense of peace that we have not previously experienced with our pressurized routines and myriad external distractions.

The history of the Zen tradition is important in understanding the subsequent influences on Zen monks and the way they lived and designed their gardens and living quarters. The deepest roots of Zen are in India, where Siddhartha Gautama was born (c. 563 BC), attained Enlightenment and founded the Buddhist religion. Japanese Zen has its origins in China, where the first Zen masters taught and the first recognizably Zen monasteries were originally founded.

Some five centuries later, this sect of Buddhism was introduced to China and over the centuries, the distinctive school of Buddhism called *Ch'an* (pronounced Zen in Japanese) evolved. Under the T'ang dynasty (618-906), also known as the Golden Age of *Ch'an*, this school gained particular eminence among artists and intellectuals and influenced their work and thought. In China's Sung period (960-1276), *Ch'an* enjoyed wider popular as well as government favour and won a following among all classes of people, spreading to Japan, Korea and Vietnam. *Ch'an* became the most powerful spiritual influence in the development of Chinese culture and *Ch'an* monasteries became leading centres of scholarship. In the words of the influential English writer on the subject, Alan Watts, "The result was a tremendous cross-fertilization of philosophical, scholarly, poetic, and artistic pursuits in which the Zen and Taoist feeling of 'naturalness' became the dominant note." The ink wash paintings of the Sung dynasty were later to have a direct influence on Japanese Zen garden design.

This *Ch'an*-inspired sensibility, in all its spiritual, cultural and artistic forms, was exported to Japan in the 11th and 12th centuries by visiting Chinese monks and by Japanese monks who had earlier travelled to China to train with *Ch'an* masters. With its austere practice and emphasis on intuition rather than learning, Zen had a particular appeal to the Japanese *samurai*, warrior classes who, in the 12th century, replaced emperors and courtiers as the country's dominant ruling elite. The Zen tradition quickly established a powerful place in the cultural and spiritual life of its new host country and, in the course of time, developed its own unique Japanese flavour.

The subsequent influence of Zen upon Japanese life and character has been profound. The Zen ideal has both led Japanese culture and provided a vehicle for manifesting inherent

Japanese values such as the love of Nature, acceptance of hardship as a pre-requisite to spiritual development, the lack of division between the religious and the secular and an understanding of the unity of beauty and ugliness, tenderness and violence, delicacy and coarseness, as manifested in the climate and landscape. Zen also brought to Japanese society a respect for tranquillity and an appreciation of maintaining peace of mind and repose in the midst of chaos and external distraction. Zen arts such as the tea ceremony and flower arranging aid cultivation of this quietude. Such mental repose allows the Japanese to find solitude on a crowded subway or within their paper-walled houses amid the noise of the external world.

Zen culture has also influenced the Japanese notion of beauty. A Zen artist finds beauty in the process of creation, or suggestion of perfection, rather than in its completion. Thus the unfinished nature of asymmetric design becomes more attractive than the order of symmetry, and this is reflected in many design features of Zen gardens and houses as well as other Japanese arts – for example, a potter with complete mastery of his technique may nevertheless choose to give his pots a rough, unfinished look.

The Zen view also corresponds with the inherent Japanese love of simplicity and lack of artifice. Unsympathetic to clutter, overdecoration or sumptuousness, the classic Japanese house, garden, kitchen utensil or cooking pot is invariably designed with clean, elegant lines demonstrating restraint and discipline and implying a depth and profundity not immediately obvious. This is especially the case with Zen stone gardens, which afford fresh insights at each visit. Japanese Zen culture also values signs of age and wear, finding beauty within them – the ravages of age demonstrating the impermanence of things while also evoking a sense of their nobility. Wooden structures, for example, are left untreated so that the patina of age created by climate or use may be seen and appreciated.

In order to fully understand the influence of the Zen tradition on the Japanese people, and vice versa, it is also important to note how the history, climate and landscape have influenced each other. These forces and those already discussed contain the origins of contemporary Japanese customs, beliefs and manners.

Until the end of the Second World War, Japan had never been successfully invaded by a foreign power, and, except for periods of openness to China in the eighth and ninth centuries and, later, to European culture and arts, the country developed in an atmosphere of isolation until the mid-19th century. Nine centuries earlier, Japan broke off all relations with the outside world and underwent two hundred years of isolation. It was during this time that the *samurai* developed as a distinct warrior class and the ethics of *bushido* (the Way of the Warrior) evolved. *Samurai* soldiers owed total allegiance to a particular local clan leader or warlord, and from the 12th to the 16th centuries, Japan was subject to almost continuous civil war. One after another, successive *shogun*, the nation's military and political leaders, remained hostile to all foreign religions and secular influences and carried out a policy of national seclusion: Japanese citizens were prohibited from travelling outside the country, while foreigners were not allowed in. The intention was to control every aspect of Japanese life in every corner of the land – where people lived, what they ate, the type of clothes they wore, even the posture they adopted and the way they slept – all were dictated by the state. The arts continued to flourish, however, and life was relatively peaceful for commoners so long as they obeyed the rules.

During the 18th and 19th centuries, the *samurai* had little to do since there were few battles to fight, yet they remained a privileged group and were expected to set a good example for the rest of society and to lead sober and honest lives. In this time of peace, the practice of the martial arts slowly became a vehicle

below: A large, hanging Buddhist temple bell (*tsurigane* or *bonsho*) which produces a deep, resonating tone. Temple bells are struck for religious functions and after making an offering.

above: A wood block print from his *Fifty-three Stages of the Tokaido* collection, by Hiroshige (1797-1858). This famous Zen-inspired artist influenced Manet and Van Gogh, among other European painters.

below: Cherry blossom is the national flower of Japan. During the few days each year when the trees are in full bloom, the Japanese gather at traditional viewing sites to enjoy the blossom and to celebrate and mourn the passing of the seasons.

right: A naturally heated (volcanic) open-air hot spring (an *onsen*). The Japanese lay great emphasis on purification and cleanliness for physical and spiritual regeneration, but the communal bath is also a place to meet, share gossip and jokes and soak away aches and pains. Heaven and earth meet in the tub.

left: For earlier generations of Japanese, one outcome of the inaccessiblity of their mountain landscapes and features such as this deep river gorge high in the Japanese Alps was to lend them an air of mystery. These were places to contemplate rather than to explore. Appreciation of natural scenery became focused on particular views rather than sweeping panoramas.

through which a *samurai* could express his understanding of Zen ideals, and the influence of the *samurai* ensured that Zen tradition permeated Japanese society.

The historical impact of Zen on the design of traditional Japanese houses and gardens has been as important as the influences of climate, landscape and the native religion, Shintoism.

In general, the climate of Japan resembles the temperate climate of the east coast of the United States, although the sub-tropical southern island of Kyushu is warmer, and the snowy, northern island of Hokkaido is colder. There are four distinct seasons. Spring begins in March (early April in northern Honshu and Hokkaido) and lasts until the beginning of June. April and May are warm and dry months. From late March to mid-April the cherry blossom ripens northwards from Kyushu to Hokkaido. The summer and rainy seasons start in early June – a hot and humid time (except in Hokkaido). From mid-July to early September, it remains hot but not wet. Mountain areas are refreshing at this time of the year. Autumn is a time of clear skies and comfortable temperatures, although late September can be wet. Winter in the north and at high altitudes is cold, snowy and beautiful; in other areas, the temperature rarely drops below freezing.

Japan's climate is heavily influenced by its mountainous terrain and indeed this is predominantly a land of mountains. The country's four main islands may, in fact, themselves be considered as the visible peaks of a deeply submerged mountain range. The mountains, some of them volcanic, can rise to 4,000 m (over 13,000 ft), while their slopes are steep and densely forested to the summits and the valleys between them deep and narrow. As a result, the population is densely confined to coastal plains and a few wide river valleys. Japan also lies directly along fault lines which mark the juxtaposition between the Pacific and Asian tectonic plates, subterranean structures which grind against each other and cause earthquakes. Submarine earthquakes produce tidal waves which regularly pound the coasts of Japan. Add to

these perils typhoon winds that occasionally savage the land, heavy snowfalls in the north, torrential summer rainstorms in the south, the heavy humid heat of central and western Honshu and Kyushu, and one can understand the role of climate and landscape in the psyche of the Japanese and its influence on their way of life. With regard to garden and house design, their importance lies in three main areas.

Firstly, the inaccessibility of the mountains has always lent them an air of mystery. These were places to contemplate rather than to explore and the Japanese appreciation of natural scenery has, out of necessity, been focussed on particular views rather than on sweeping panoramas. Secondly, within the confines of high-density living, small gardens were designed as distillations of the natural world, giving an impression of a large-scale landscape. Both factors had a direct impact on later garden design. Thirdly, the nature of Japan's climate and the possibility at any time of destruction by earthquake or typhoon imposed contrasting restrictions on the Japanese home. The need for protection from extremes of weather had to be matched with a choice of design and materials that allowed fast reconstruction in the event of extreme weather damage. Simple design and the use of a small range of local materials such as unpainted wood, stones, rice paper, bark and straw, offered a solution.

Wood, therefore, with which Japan is blessed in abundance, is the structural building material best suited to the humid climate and the ever-present risk of earthquake. Different varieties of wood, together with paper, are also used to construct many of the interior features of the Japanese house such as *shoji* screens, lampshades and bases and the typical communal bathtubs. The tradition of using untreated natural materials has been used by Zen-inspired architects to create an unpretentious style of house, in keeping with the landscape and climate, and is much admired within the Zen tradition.

Followers of Shinto, the native religion of Japan, worship

myriad gods (collectively known as *kami*), who are perceived to be embodied in all manner of natural phenomena such as rivers, mountains, rocks and trees. A particularly old tree or interestingly shaped rock or, on a larger scale, a mountain (Mount Fuji especially) became sacred objects of worship, and the spirits within them were appealed to for good health or a successful harvest, and so on. To approach such a sacred object, the worshipper requires purification with water and at a Shinto shrine, water is inevitably provided for worshippers to use for the symbolic cleansing of their hands and mouths. The appreciation of objects found in Nature such as rocks and the importance of the symbolism of water later became characteristic features of Zen gardens, while the design of Shinto nature shrines, especially the importance of integrating architecture and setting, was also to have an influence on the design of residential architecture.

I owe much of my understanding of the architecture of the Japanese home to Richard Smith, an American architect who lived in Japan for many years. His view of what we can learn from the traditional house is most instructive:

"Perhaps the greatest lesson of the Japanese house is to remind us that we, in the West, have distanced ourselves from a more natural and healthy place in the world. The industrialization of virtually all aspects of life and our apparent desire to manifest every new technological or scientific idea or advance in the fabric of the home, may play a larger role in our health and well-being than we dare think."

Modern Japanese buildings are, unfortunately, no more or less environmentally friendly than their western counterparts. With reference to modern environmental and health concerns, however, the classic, traditional Japanese house still found in older districts of cities and in the countryside provides an excellent working model. It is built from a limited palette of readily available materials, thus reducing the need for reliance on industrial processes and transportation with their attendant envi-

ronmental pollution. Zen respect for the transformation of natural materials through weathering and age removes the need for surface embellishment and preservation and the toxins they can produce. The use of room dividers and sliding outdoor screens provides a healthy response to climate. In the summer all sliding panels can be opened or removed, encouraging the flow of fresh air throughout the house. In wintertime, the interior of the house can be converted into an arrangement of individual rooms which can be closed off from each other and the outside.

The Japanese way of bathing, in addition to making a contribution of its own to personal cleanliness and good health, is another way of keeping warm and conserving body heat. The *ofuro* (bathtub) is a relatively deep and short bath. The water is heated by its own boiler, usually located outside the house. You wash thoroughly before entering the tub, sometimes with others, to soak. The bath water is, therefore, kept clean, reused and reheated when necessary. Sometimes, boards are floated to insulate the water and prevent heat loss. More often, a wooden board is used as a lid.

Classic Japanese houses were designed to attend as closely to a man's inner needs as to his physical comfort, and evolved as a result of influences already discussed, and from a blending of two sources. The initial inspiration was a style of architecture known as *Kara-yo,* introduced to Japan from China in the 13th century. *Kara-yo* was the official style of building used in China during the Sung period and was itself derived from the architecture of *Ch'an* monasteries and aristocratic mansions. The other influence, and the one that gave the Japanese house its most definitive characteristics, was the alliance of Zen and *samurai* ideals. Zen priests and the *samurai* warriors who controlled the country had much in common, for each prized austerity, frugality, self-discipline and boldness of spirit. In the design of their own living quarters, they brought these virtues to bear on *Kara-yo*-style architecture. The result of the fusion was what became

left: A Japanese bathtub or *ofuro,* in which the water is kept clean, reheated and reused. The Zen tradition of using untreated, natural materials creates an unpretentious look.

below: Typical Japanese rooms are simple and multi-functional. The *futon* bed (stowed away in the daytime) is laid directly onto *tatami* mats. *Shoji* screens control ventilation and give access to the verandah, framing the view.

known as the *Shoin*-style house, characterized by open space, clean lines and rectangular shapes, and harmony between interior privacy and openness to Nature. The *Shoin* style was originally used in *samurai* mansions and the private quarters of Zen abbots, though, in the Edo period (1600-1868), it was adapted for their own use on a smaller scale by urban merchants and artisans. They maintained the basic *Shoin* elements such as the *tokonoma* (a decorative alcove), *tatami* (floor mats), *fusuma* (paper doors) and *shoji* (sliding doors).

Fusuma are opaque, padded paper doors which sometimes have decorative paintings on them, while *shoji* screens – sliding translucent panels – are used to separate rooms from exterior spaces. They create the inner room partitions and the outer house screen walls, but serve no structural purpose. The interior of a Japanese home is a functionally free space which may be divided into a variety of areas by closing, opening or removing the screens according to how a room is to be used. Outside screens may be opened or closed to bring into view the garden or change the ventilation in the house.

Tatami mats, made of woven straw, cover the floors wall-to-wall and are used to sit and sleep on. Chairs are not used and to keep the floor clean, street shoes are left at the *genkan*, an entrance-hall or vestibule which acts as a barrier between the dust of the street and the interior of the house.

Another feature of a traditional house is the *engawa*, a verandah and walkway protected by an overhanging roof. This acts as an intermediate space between the home and garden and softens the division between people and Nature. This relationship between interior and garden consciously parallels the Zen view, identifying the external world as an extension of our inner life.

The *tokonoma* is an alcove with a raised platform used for the display of art, usually a very special flower arrangement or an ink wash painting, normally monochrome to blend with the soft tones of the room. Flower arranging (in Japanese, *ikebana*) is a

way of presenting seasonal flowers and other plants in vases according to prescribed rules and has developed into a sophisticated art form in Japan. The *tokonoma* is the traditional show place for demonstrating *ikebana* floral arrangements.

The *Shoin* style was later influenced in the 16th century by the development of tea house architecture, itself guided by a set of rules devised to govern the tea ceremony. They were created by Sen no Rikyu (1521-1591). A tea master and advisor on matters of aesthetics to powerful men, it was he who established the four principles for enacting the tea ceremony: harmony, reverence, purity and silence. For the ceremony's setting in the tea house, he stressed simplicity and rusticity within a framework of beauty and naturalness. *Shoin* style was influenced by the humble tea houses and this amalgamation gave rise to *Sukiya* style, which in turn evolved into what is now understood to be the traditional Japanese dwelling.

The impact of the Zen view on Japanese garden construction is first associated with an early technical treatise, the *Enposho* or *Book of Gardens* (also known as *Senzui Narabini Yagyuzo*, publication date unknown). Attributed to the Shingon Buddhist priest Zoen, it is one of Japan's most influential books on garden design and emphasizes tranquillity and harmony rather than variety and decorative qualities. This legacy was developed by later monks within the Zen tradition and many of Japan's most celebrated gardens were subsequently designed by Zen priests and created within the grounds of Zen monasteries and temples. Here, they provided the monks with a contemplative, everyday work activity, an aesthetic experience, and a place of natural beauty.

Compared to its western counterpart, the classic Zen garden was subdued, with a stress on asymmetry and spatial harmony rather than symmetry and geometric form. Economy of means and materials was another characteristic of the traditional Zen garden. The basic components – rocks, sand, water, trees, shrubs, ferns and moss – were used to represent mountains,

below: A view of Ritsurin Park, Taka-matsu, Shikoku, a stroll garden designed to be walked around. The use of the wooded hillside (called *shakkei* or "borrowed scenery") visually enlarges the scale and variety of the garden.

right: Part of a raked gravel garden with naturally sculpted stones. The pine tree has been pruned to recreate its natural wind-ravaged form. The combination of natural shapes and control by the gardener is typical of Japanese garden design.

below: A traditional "rustic" teahouse, constructed in a setting that is a recreation of a typical Japanese mountain location or hermit's hideaway.

Tea gardens imitate the tranquillity of the deep mountains and feature mainly evergreen trees and shrubs.

rivers, oceans and waterfalls to create scenic landscapes in miniature, and maintenance of the garden became a vehicle for daily Zen work practice. This is exemplified in the story of the young novice Zen monk who, when told to tidy a garden, asked his master where he should throw the rubbish. "Where is the rubbish?" asked the master, as he took broken twigs and leaves for kindling and carried small stones to catch rain drops from the eaves, leaving only a small pile of dust and gravel which he raked back into the garden – a basic lesson in conservation for us all!

Three main styles of Japanese garden have evolved. Each has been influenced by three design factors: the Zen view, the designs for Japanese gardens which predated Zen, and the natural landscape at hand. They are known as the *tsukiyama* (landscape garden), the *karesansui* (rock garden style) and the *chaniwa* (tea garden).

Tsukiyama gardens typically feature streams with stepping stones and a bridge leading to a small island set in a pond. A twisting path leads the visitor from one feature to another, so that various changing scenes can be viewed. Some gardens feature miniaturized versions of actual beauty spots famous in Japanese art or literature.

In the *karesansui* or rock garden style (also called dry stone landscape gardens), the gardens are designed, like a painting, for contemplation. Few shrubs are used and the most common elements are stones, sand and gravel. Historically, several of the best Zen gardeners were also well-known painters who with just a few strokes of black ink on white paper could evoke an atmospheric natural scene. Their gardens were three-dimensional interpretations of that idea, but they used sand or gravel instead of paper or silk, and shrubs, trees or stones in place of brush strokes. The stones they chose were also charged with different meanings according to their shapes, their textures and the angles at which they were placed. The garden at Ryoan-ji Temple, Kyoto (completed around the beginning of the 16th century) is

generally recognized as one of the finest examples of a *karesansui* in Japan. The abstract design of the garden is said to be a physical representation of the relationship between being and non-being (in Zen parlance: between form and emptiness).

The third style, the *chaniwa*, is a small garden planted around a teahouse to enable visitors to prepare for and enhance their experience of the peaceful, spiritual tea ceremony. This formal ritual for preparing and drinking green tea originated in Chinese Buddhist temples and was later refined by Japanese Zen monks. The ceremony cultivates inner calm and the appreciation of the beauty of Nature. A tea garden looks simple and natural, but the intention behind the design of the path leading through it, the views presented of the teahouse and the composition of the plants compress the experience of walking from home in town to the mountain hideaway of a hermit. The design principles of the *chaniwa* were the same as those that governed the tea ceremony itself. In a passage from his book, *Zen Culture*, Thomas Hoover evokes perfectly the relationship between man and the Japanese house and garden:

"As the guest kneels on the cushions and sips green tea, the host may slide aside a rear shoji *to reveal the roofless garden of the inner courtyard, his private abstraction of the natural landscape. Flowers are purposely absent, but in their place may be tiny, shaped pines, a pond, and receding, rocky pathways. The mossy stones glisten with dew (or with water from a recent dousing by the host in preparation for his guests), and the air is fresh with the scent of greenery. Only upon careful inspection does the deception evaporate and the garden reveal itself to be a tiny plot surrounded by a bamboo and plaster fence; the natural world has been extracted and encapsulated into a single view, at once as authentic as the forest and as artfully detailed as a Flemish miniature. This view – a heritage of Zen* Shoin *design – is vital to the aesthetic magic of the house, for it brings the works of man and nature together in a way that blurs their distinction."*

interiors

"... abandoning worldliness, I often come to this tranquil place –

The spirit here is the spirit of Zen."

From **Truly I Love This Life of Seclusion**

RYOKAN (c. 1758 – 1831)

For centuries, Zen Buddhism has informed and shaped every aspect of Japanese society; what Westerners see as "typically Japanese" has its roots in the philosophy and aesthetics of Zen.

above: Running water is symbolic of clarity and purity, and is a feature much found in Zen-style buildings and their surroundings, whether in Japan or the West.

Its characteristic timeless, apparent simplicity is the reason for its continuing appeal. Zen-style interiors are places where inhabitants have created a haven of peace and calm. The overall emphasis on simplicity is integral to Zen, which teaches that it is possible to hone down the clutter and extraneous matter of everyday life, to create a clear, ordered setting to allow a free rein, mentally, physically and spiritually.

The apparent austerity of Zen-style interiors relies on intuition, insight and concentration. It is not intellectual, but it is intelligent. Zen Buddhism has been defined as "vast emptiness"; the anti-materialistic aspects of the philosophy are well-known, but this is only one facet. Zen practitioners believe in the use of the best possible materials in the most harmonious interiors. Overt displays of wealth, ostentation or conspicuous consumption are replaced by a sense of the aesthetic pleasure in the natural world, the changing season, or the representation of Nature in microcosm to be found in the traditional Japanese garden. The Zen lifestyle is fluid, advocating the creation of tranquil, interpenetrating spaces yet flexible enough to change the atmosphere and the function of an interior using the practical measures inherent to traditional Japanese lifestyles. Zen addresses both inner needs and physical comforts, with clean lines and rectilinearity, subdued economy of form and elimination of the unnecessary. Zen is not aesthetically frugal or impoverished, but its visual vocabulary, *shibui*, cultivates an apparent austerity of taste and is perfectly in keeping with the central themes of Millennial Modernism, the eclectic international style which blends Modernist elements and those of other cultures. Zen enthusiasts recognise that it is easier to live coherently and to think creatively in an environment which allows the inhabitants to deal with the flotsam and jetsam of everyday life. Clarity of vision allows one to focus on the important, rather than on the immediate.

Western Zen-influenced interiors may seem to be sparse, empty of decoration and over-designed, but this is deceptive. Like Zen itself, this "editing" is not a matter of barring the outside world in order to live in a hermetically sealed monastic cell. Zen is not elitist, but thoughtful and profound; it is not simple, but rather a distinction between the essential and the disposable.

Great western architects of the 20th century instinctively recognised solutions to their own pressing problems. The manipulation of interpenetrating space typical of Frank Lloyd Wright's domestic architecture is directly attributable to his knowledge of Japanese buildings; the interplay between house and landscape, which Wright called "organic architecture", reflects Buddhist philosophies about the function of the house and its relationship with its surroundings. Modernists appreciated the clean lines, the lack of meaningless decoration, and the ordered, fluid interiors of Zen-influenced buildings, while the Organic Movement practitioners used natural materials, colours and shapes to evoke the outside world. Building a house to take the best advantage of how sunlight changes during the course of the day, transforming the interior with the passing of the seasons and "blurring the boundaries" between internal and external are now intrinsic elements of the western architectural vocabulary. What we assume to be progressive, forward-thinking developments are, in fact, centuries-old Japanese principles, and deeply rooted in Zen.

left: In a minimalist western apartment, the elements of wood, stone and fire are carefully articulated to symbolize the dependence of the man-made world on the natural.

right: A collection of visually appealing natural forms is used here as a "still life", provoking contemplation. Such arrangements take the place of ornate decoration or ornaments usually found in traditional European interiors.

in conditions of enforced intimacy which would amaze all but the most sociable Westerner. Consequently, great emphasis is laid upon the way in which an interior can be quickly and easily converted from a succession of interlocking boxes affording a modicum of privacy to a comparatively large open space, by the use of partitions. Perhaps the best known of these are the *fusuma*, pairs of which run in parallel wooden tracks located in the floor and below the lintel. A lightweight wooden frame, only 1.5 centimetres (⅝ inch) thick, is covered with opaque textured paper, and fitted with a recessed handle to avoid tearing or marking the corresponding *fusuma* when slid one on top of the other. *Fusuma* can easily be slid out of their tracks and stored elsewhere when not required. Conversely, lightweight folding screens are also employed, when needed, to reduce the space, to create a feeling of intimacy and to block draughts. They are often deployed around *futon*, the traditional soft cotton fibre-filled mattress of Japan, which is still very popular. Unlike western beds, which are used for about 8 hours a day but otherwise occupy valuable space for the other 16 hours, *futon* and their top quilts, which are very like duvets, are folded up and stored in cupboards when not required. What had been a bedroom becomes a living room in a matter of minutes. *Futon* are infinitely flexible; when the weather is particularly cold they are piled on top of one another to give extra insulation under the sleeper. If a household has an extra number of guests to stay overnight, spare *futon* can be borrowed from the neighbours – not a realistic option in a society committed to the sprung mattress.

In Japan, *futon* are placed straight on the floor – or rather, they are placed on *tatami* matting. Individual mats cover the entire surface of a room and therefore one can sit or sleep anywhere in a *tatami* matted room. *Tatami* is not so much a floor covering as an infinitely flexible form of furnishing, and removes the need for the serried ranks of furniture found in western settings. Matching square floor cushions called *zabuton* are

provided to make sitting, kneeling or reclining more comfortable. Such furniture as there is tends to be low-level and unobtrusive, lightweight and foldable so that it can be stored when not in use. The central role played by the dining or kitchen table in the west is taken by the *kotatsu* in Japan. A low-level square table resting on four legs, the *kotatsu* is used for family dining, homework, receiving visitors, a forum for gossip and the centre of family life. But this is no ordinary table – the tabletop actually rests on a wooden frame and can be lifted off so that in cold weather a very large, square, padded quilt (a *kotatsu futon*) can be draped over the frame and be held in place by the replaced tabletop. There is an electrical heating element on the underside and when this is switched on the family can sit around the *kotatsu* draped to the waist in a warm quilt. When it is time for spring cleaning, the *kotatsu* can be dismantled and stored in a cupboard till required again. Each piece of traditional furniture has a double function, and, as far as possible, each piece folds, stacks or dismantles when not in use, to maximize space. Contemporary Japanese designers draw on their Zen roots to provide adaptable, space-saving solutions to the problems of living in a small apartment or house. For example, the traditional form of the household *butsudan* or miniature domestic Buddhist altar is that of a tall, slim, discreetly lacquered cabinet, fronted by double doors. When opened up, the doors of the *butsudan* fold outwards to reveal an interior of magnificent workmanship, glowing colour and symbolic complexity. The *butsudan* functions as a focal point for prayers and offerings, and as a private source of spiritual renewal. But when not in use, the *butsudan* recedes quietly and unobtrusively into the background. The compact, double-doored "Schrein", a combined folding work station and piece of furniture for storage designed by Masayuki Kurokawa, echoes both the physical form of the *butsudan* and many of its chameleon-like qualities. Shelves, filing space and a dual layer workstation are all concealed behind discreet hinged doors set

opposite:
Sliding translucent screens conceal the bedroom area in a small studio apartment, creating a flexible space which is both comfortable and intimate.

left: The provision of a fixed island unit articulates the kitchen and dining areas without blocking them off from one another; the "work" areas of the relatively compact kitchen are hidden from view yet accessible, and the room divider functions as both dining table and extra workspace.

into a compact cabinet on castors, providing the perfect personal office for small apartments. Similarly, the mobile kitchen unit designed by Masanori Umeda is a single, articulated, rectangular block which is laid out in an enclosed cabinet like a child's toy theatre or a doll's house. When the "wings" are folded back, this astonishing, space-saving design is seen to house a stove, a hob, a sink, a refrigerator and a dishwasher, as well as ample worktops for food preparation. The whole unit is mounted on castors and when not in use can be disconnected from the utilities' sources, folded up and successfully ignored – if necessary, the entire "kitchen" can be moved from one setting to another, a specific homage to the portable *tansu* or storage chests of earlier times.

It is important to remember that during Japan's pre-industrialized era of total seclusion from the outside world, the forms of man-made objects and interiors were primarily dictated by their function and both reliant upon and measured against the design concepts of previous generations. The absence of new technologies and materials and the lack of external influences during the

left: The successful articulation of space in a small domestic setting is vital to the creation of an adaptable, flexible home. Here, the unified flooring scheme maintains visual continuity throughout the space, while hinged partitions act as screens between the bedroom and living areas.

left: Two views of the same interior; sliding screens with recessed handles run in tracks at lintel and floor level, subdividing the seating and dining areas without separating them.

below: Unobtrusive, low-level furniture is arranged to give a view over the garden, which is both visible and accessible through the sliding glass doors. The partition wall of glass bricks allows light into the interior and consciously echoes the grid effect of *shoji* screens.

two hundred years of isolation meant that aesthetic and practical developments were evolutionary, rather than revolutionary, cautious and gradual rather than rapid or innovative. Any display of rampant individualism would also have met with official disapproval and social ostracism; a popular Japanese proverb of the time was "The nail which sticks up gets hammered down", a salutary warning against hubris, egotism, personal ambition or eccentricity. However, in the second half of this century the Japanese have adopted and adapted so many new ways of living, from international fashions to fast foods, from high-tech building materials to the celebration of Valentine's Day, that a modern-day Japanese insult is to describe someone as being "like a frog in a well", succinctly dismissing them as hidebound, blinkered and rigid in attitude. Social adaptability and openness to new ideas have come to be seen as progressive and forward-looking – ideal for the new millenium.

opposite and left: The masterful interplay of space in this minimalist interior creates a feeling of tranquillity and flexibility; the overall rectilinear effect is softened by the thoughtful juxtaposition of much-loved artworks as focal points for contemplation.

right: An entire wall of storage is concealed by sliding doors and topped with a library on open shelves; in an otherwise empty space, the chair – a twentieth-century design classic – takes on a sculptural significance.

s i m p l i c i t y

Zen is often perceived by the outside world as being austere, doctrinaire and harsh. Certainly, for novice monks, their early years are rigorous and disciplined, but Zen does not propound frugality and anti-materialism as ends in themselves, but rather as ways to clear the mind in order to work towards *satori* or enlightenment.

above: The cultivation of studied simplicity relies upon the ability to conceal from view what is not immediately required. In this bathroom, the washbasin and shaving mirror are hidden behind sliding doors when not required.

The apparent austerity of spirit or astringency of taste is exemplified in the Japanese term *shibui*. This concept is inherent to Zen and has become an integral part of Japanese aesthetics. *Shibui* stands for "poverty of taste", for the absence of ostentatious detail or superfluous ornament, a cultivation of the minimal, an appreciation of the integrity of materials. *Shibui* does not spurn comfort or aesthetic pleasure – instead it highlights the importance of quality and truth to materials in all aspects of everyday life. At its most basic level, this translates as the belief that an individual has the power of choice – and that one should consciously choose the best quality, the most comfortable, the most perfectly suited to one's needs and the most expressive of commitment to simplicity.

To understand the fundamental principle of cultivated simplicity in Japanese life, it is important to consider that for more than two centuries, until the 1860s, every aspect of human life was rigorously controlled by a rigid set of laws known as the "Sumptuary Edicts", imposed by the Tokugawa Shogunate, the hereditary government. Society was run under feudal lines with a strict hierarchy. As well as defining the precise place of every individual within the hierarchical pyramid and therefore restricting the choices of who they might marry or where they might live, the "Sumptuary Edicts" controlled the most minute details of everyday life. Under these laws, regardless of an individual's income, they were restricted to the social class into which they were born for their entire lives. Every aspect of their conduct and consumption was detailed and

restricted, ruthlessly dictated by law. For example, a family classified as "small rice farmers" would work their whole lives without ever tasting their staple crop. They would be forbidden to wear robust wooden clogs but would be forced to wear inferior straw sandals, would have to sleep on clay floors rather than wood or *tatami* mats, and would have to wear simple robes made from indigo-dyed cotton decorated only with a small geometric motif. Regardless of income, any social aspirations, desire for experimentation or self-expression was denied – punishment for infringing the rules meant at least social ostracism and public ridicule and, at worst, a summary death for anyone transgressing the strict boundaries of decent behaviour.

Two hundred years of enforced simplicity and frugality created a weird dichotomy in the national psyche – an understandable aversion to anything which smacked of conspicuous consumption, ostentation or personal vanity. Conversely, an overriding respect developed for excellence of manufacture and materials in even the humblest, everyday artefact. Even today the Japanese take a great deal of pleasure in the simplest detail; the perfectly cooked bowl of rice is a measure of the cook's skill and it is imperative to praise the plain bowl of rice which arrives at the end of every sumptuous, intricate meal. This attention to detail is seen in every social situation, from the consummate skill required to correctly phrase and hand-write a New Year's greeting card to one's family doctor or line manager, to the packaging of five fresh eggs on market

left: This dining room exemplifies the Zen concept of *shibui*, with its absence of ostentatious decoration and ornament and its apparent austerity of taste. Great attention has been paid to the selection of furniture which expresses the nature of its component materials.

left: We tend to see the bathroom as a room with a specific function, but it can also be made aesthetically appealing by the emphasis on unadorned wood, complying with the notion of *wabi* or truth to materials.

right: A flexible system of wooden wall-pegs at regular intervals allows the bather to reach everything required quite easily; functional and user-friendly, this ease of access has obvious parallels in the Shaker approach to interior design.

stalls in a hand-woven rigid net of straw. All are evidence of the need to perform even the humblest task with the greatest attention to detail, and expressive of the general appreciation of "small things well-done".

To the Japanese, the term "simplicity" does not have the slightly dismissive or even derisive connotations it retains in the West, where it can be a synonym for "unsophisticated" or "lacking artifice". Paradoxically, what we superficially call "simple" often appears to the Japanese to be highly sophisticated so long as it conforms to the Zen aesthetic of *shibui,* austerity or astringency of taste, a concept reinterpreted by Frank Lloyd Wright as "the elimination of the insignificant". The absence of florid colour, inappropriate or badly applied decoration or clumsy attempts to mask or conceal the true nature of an object adds integrity and a sense of worth to even the humblest artefact. An unostentatious design in which integrity and efficiency of function merge is seen by many Japanese as being an expression of consummate skill. Part of the appeal lies in the recognition of what has been rigorously excluded. This approach, which complies with the abstract notion of "vast emptiness", so central to Buddhism, also occurs in the resonant silences between staccato notes in Japanese classical music; the absence of sound is perceived to be as haunting and evocative as the notes or chords themselves. The profound longueurs in classical Noh theatre also create a heightened sense of tension and again,

above: In its reduction to pure essentials,
the Zen-style bathroom is the epitome of
sensual minimalism: natural light filters
through a translucent blind and the sinuous
forms of an exotic flowering plant become
a focus for contemplation.

it is the occasional apparent absence of action or sound which augments the drama.

The absence of frivolity or artifice and the recognition of austerity of taste is epitomized in the Zen concept of *wabi* or "truth to materials", and is celebrated in the creation of hand-crafted ceramics. Their typical characteristics include deliberate "imperfections" in shape and form, the irregularity or apparent casualness of minimalist decoration, and a reliance on the texture of the raw material through the use of subtle glazes and rough finishes. In this century, Japanese ceramicists such as Shoji Hamada and Soetsu Yanagi have returned to and revitalised the central Zen principles of *wabi*, and their work has influenced western potters such as the late Bernard Leach and Lucie Rie, who also created works of great dignity through their "simple" and timeless designs.

It is remarkable to observe the tenacity of traditional aesthetic values and the philosophies of Zen which continue to govern the conception and creation of man-made objects, interiors and structures.

The desire for simplicity and the appreciation of the way in which it can enhance the quality of life is apparent in the centuries-old philosophy behind the creation of the traditional Japanese house. Novelist Junichiro Tanizaki half-jokingly stated that "When we plan to build a house we first put up a parasol – and in the shade we build a house." The image of the house as merely a temporary shelter is intrinsic to Japanese interpretations of Buddhism. The Buddha achieved enlightenment while sitting in the shade under a tree, and this concept of striving for *satori* in a temporary shelter has informed Japanese approaches to the creation of domestic architecture, which is typically modest, unobtrusive, infinitely flexible yet intimately linked with the surrounding natural world, expressed through the use of unadorned natural materials, neutral earthy colours and an emphasis upon the skeletal elements of the structure.

There are practical reasons for the apparent simplicity of the Japanese house; a feudal society whose members were actively discouraged from travelling within their own country and who were shut off from foreign influences for two centuries were forced to use indigenous, local skills and manpower to design and construct any building.

Architecture in its western sense was largely unknown outside the upper classes of society, and vernacular builders therefore relied upon past construction practices and the raw materials available locally to create homes for themselves. Her-metically sealed from foreign fads and fashions, such as those which continuously swept Europe and America in the 18th and 19th century, the Japanese developed a profoundly indigenous vernacular style of building which was founded in their interpre-tation of Buddhism and which did not trumpet personal wealth or social aspirations.

The interior of a traditional Japanese house is also expressive of Zen ideals. Certain rooms have well-defined functions – kitchens are seen as workplaces with a specific role, and all fittings and fixtures within them are designed to work effectively. Unlike in the West, kitchens tend to be small and are not seen as a "living room", but rather as a workroom. Bathrooms are also slightly different – the bathroom is seen as a place for spiritual refreshment as well as a place to get clean. Toilets are always separated from the bathroom itself to meet ideas of hygiene. However, all other rooms are seen as "living rooms", flexible, open, and unencumbered.

The Zen interior is an interconnected sequence of fluid spaces, with a studied neutrality of function, each room being seen as a blank canvas, endlessly adaptable and flexible according to the varying needs of the inhabitants. The concept of personal privacy so intrinsic to Westerners is alien to a society which places the welfare of the group before that of the individ-ual, and, as a result, space is seen as luxury.

above:
Functional and visually appealing, this simple teapot exemplifies the traditional Zen concept of *wabi*, truth to materials. Even the humblest everyday object should appeal to the senses and be as well-suited to its purpose as possible.

To achieve an impression of space in what is actually a really very small home, it is necessary to cultivate a clear, uncluttered environment. The Zen-inspired interior looks minimalist but in fact it is almost sensuous in its attention to detail and to the quality of its materials, finishes and textures. *Wabi*, the idea of truth to materials, is an inherently Zen concept and it states that everyday objects should reveal both the nature of their materials and their proper function. In practice this means an emphasis upon revealing rather than concealing the natural grain of wood, the texture of plaster, the colours of stone.

Anything not immediately required is concealed or excluded from the domestic landscape, from *futon* and folding chairs to footwear, homework to hair dryers. An often overlooked feature of Zen-style interiors is the importance of storage space to accommodate the impedimenta of everyday life. In pre-industrial Japan, the practice of storing possessions not in immediate use has its roots in the social necessity of hiding the evidence of wealth and consumption, and it is interesting that one feature of Zen-inspired interiors in the West today is the absence of easily-recognisable clues to the social status or personal wealth of the occupants. The apparent democracy of Zen-inspired domestic interiors may well be a factor in their popularity in the West.

Furniture is also often minimal, both in quantity and in size, to achieve a feeling of lightness and space. In Japanese interiors furniture is often low-level as the floor is the social arena, but this usually does not suit Westerners unaccustomed from infancy to sitting cross-legged or kneeling for hours on end. Instead, designers tend to reduce the number of pieces of furniture in a setting but to make them multi-functional, so that a single large table becomes the focal point of the room as the setting for eating, working, talking. Some Zen practitioners, such as the British architect John Pawson, achieve a unique solution to this problem by creating furniture which is almost a sculptural, structural element in the interior; profoundly simple, almost monolithic tables, benches or low shelves are designed as an integral part of the interior.

The Zen approach is evident in the studied neutrality of many contemporary Japanese architects and designers, and their work has been highly influential in the West. Tadao Ando limits his architectural vocabulary to relatively few materials and surface treatments, such as plate glass, polished concrete and unadorned wood. While his materials are unashamedly modern, relatively humble and perhaps surprisingly unpretentious, he insists on the highest possible standards of quality in workmanship and finish. Ando pursues excellence in all designed objects, particularly in their functional capacity and adaptability, in order to create rigorously minimalist yet individualistic buildings and interiors. Similarly, designer Shigeru Uchida eliminates the superfluous and calls the resulting style Modern Stoic. One of his most famous and internationally influential commissions is the U Atelier, an abstract simplification of the dwelling space, finished in Japanese pine and lauan plywood.

Uchida describes the project as essentially "a rectangular room which contains only two 'objects', which are raised from the floor. One serves as a table, the other serves as a kind of sitting space. Since neither is attached to the structure, both of these are functional. What is important in U Atelier is that the 'objects' are not perceived as furnishings. They create function and psychologically divide the space."

Uchida employs very traditional Japanese methods in that in his interiors, space is delineated only by the bare minimum of disparate objects; large-scale, multi-functional components suggest or cater for, rather than dictate, the activities of the inhabitants. The ceiling above the table is pierced by a giant skylight, giving glimpses of the forest and providing daylight and warmth to the people sitting below. Conversely, the seating or sleeping platform is almost cosy and intimate by comparison – a dichotomy defined by the designer as "cool warmth".

In all his projects, Uchida begins by considering the floor, which, he believes, "supports an invisible space above it. I find the floor to be the most important element in defining space" – a further indication of his cultural debt to indigenous philosophies and practices. To use his own words, "the true principle of interiors lies in the spiritual side of our everyday lives."

An underlying sense of spirituality is the key to understanding the apparent simplicity of the Zen interior. The provision of space or void and the absence of decoration are not perceived as a "lack" in Japanese aesthetics. Emptiness is seen as resonant in its own right. What is implied or left unstated is equal in significance to those elements which are both concrete and tangible. On a more practical level, the minimalism of the "simple" interior is both inexpensive to achieve and a more sensible and sensitive use of limited natural resources and materials, a design criterion likely to increase in importance in the next century.

The almost monochrome tones or muted colours of a traditional Zen interior allow the subdued hues of unadorned natural materials to glow quietly. In keeping with the Buddhist precept that the house is merely a temporary shelter, a fragile and unimposing refuge during this transitory existence, it would be considered inappropriate and vulgar to lavish brilliant colour or ostentatious decoration on the domestic setting in order to make one's home or possessions seem more important than they really are. To do so would be to invite some nemesis in the form of a flood, earthquake or fire. Consequently, the Zen-inspired interior with its chameleon-like muted colour scheme, its constantly changing internal arrangements and portable, seasonal props, becomes a flexible, neutrally coloured stage setting. Inhabitants and their guest "shine" against such a backdrop; in addition, carefully selected "worthy" objects are often emphasized by their strong colours.

These focal points are, by their very nature, transitory and interchangeable, significant for their relevance to the season, the

above: Clarity of structure is apparent in this understairs corner, and the miscellany of carefully selected sculptural forms both appeals to the eye and expresses the aesthetic tastes of the occupants.

right: Emphasis on the natural grain of wood on the floors and in the stairwell in this entrance hall creates a satisfying visual unity in what is actually a small and complex space. Built-in cupboards lining the hallway conceal all the impedimenta of everyday life. In Japanese homes, the *genkan* or lobby area, is where outdoor shoes are discarded in favour of house slippers, helping to keep the interior clean.

opposite: Reduced to flat planes of contrasting textures and surfaces, the light, neutral colour scheme of this minimalist interior evokes feelings of tranquillity and serenity.

setting or future aspirations of the household. The use of colour – or its deliberate exclusion – is seen not as an issue of mere decoration or personal whim; instead, to Zen devotees, colour has vital qualities and connotations that draw upon an established, universally understood visual language. The traditional Five Colours of Buddhist theory, which reached Japan from China at the same time as Buddhism itself, continue to have great symbolic significance.

Red implies vigour, tenacity, vivacity and celebration and therefore is much used throughout the year at times of major festivals or *matsuri*. Blue stands for tranquillity, peace, order, stability, sobriety and hard work. Yellow encompasses both gold and green; it signifies rebirth, regeneration and, not least, the natural world. Black has connotations of solemnity, mystery, and intuition and so has long-standing associations with Zen, especially when used in tandem with white, now again fashionable in the West, which symbolizes purity and spiritual aspiration.

It is interesting to note that both Oriental and Occidental interior designers working in the Modernist or Minimalist styles continue to create largely monochrome, linear, refined and austere settings, yet they choose to add key elements which are colourful, decorative, exuberant and inventive.

Zen-inspired designers are typified by their rigorous and analytical approaches and their rejection of fussy detail. The creation of an apparently "simple" environment is, in fact, a complex process, involving the careful consideration of all the materials,

forms, colours and textures to be included in order to augment the effect of the displayed items. What is more, simplicity relies on high levels of skill in craftsmanship so as not to detract from the whole. Given the information-laden, stressful nature of modern life, it is perhaps unsurprising to note the increasing popularity of empathetic, adaptable, and ostensibly simple domestic interiors.

Simplicity is a matter of paring down to the essence of things, eliminating what is superfluous. One of Buddhism's central tenets is the need to renounce all earthly, transitory desires; to abnegate personal ambition, self-will, lust, greed and vanity through living a simple, modest and productive life that is committed to hard work, group loyalty and enlightenment through meditation and contemplation.

Zen Buddhism is not a hair-shirt philosophy and takes no particular pleasure in abstention, self-denial or self-righteous frugality. However, it advocates the cultivation of personal insight through the elimination of the unnecessary which allow one to focus on what is important rather than what is immediately apparent.

Clarity of mind is aided by a quiet, tranquil, flexible environment. Simplicity is conducive, even crucial, to concentration on what is vital, life-enhancing, productive and pleasurable. Accordingly, "simplicity" in the Zen sense is anything but "simple", as the term is understood in the West; instead it is a profound and sophisticated philosophical concept.

above: Unassuming in form and expressive of their function, Edmund de Waal's ceramics exemplify the notions of "truth to materials" and "austerity of taste", which have their roots in the Zen philosophy.

left: The *kaidan tansu* or stepped storage chest of rural Japan was originally designed to be used as stairs to the next floor. These chests are now highly prized by collectors for their sculptural appeal. Sets of stacking boxes provide neat, portable storage for smaller items; when not in use they can nest inside one another to save space.

opposite: Here, the recesses cut into a false wall accommodates essential kitchen equipment. The overall visual effect is one of unity and clarity of purpose.

Tansu were used to store valuables, documents and money as well as objects of considerable beauty which it was neither socially acceptable nor wise to have on open display.

Kaidan tansu, a traditional stepped chest designed to be used as stairs in more affluent rural homes, offered drawers of variable size and depth to hold a family's many belongings. Now much sought after by collectors in the Far East and overseas, *kaidan tansu* are appreciated for both their monolithic, sculptural appeal and their original, dual function as both stairs and storage space.

For smaller items, precious ceramics, artworks or books, boxes and containers offer flexible methods of storage. Boxes of all sizes and shapes are a regular feature of Japanese life – even the humblest gift often comes beautifully packaged, occasionally in a small, handmade wooden box with a tightly fitting lid which will protect the contents from extremes of temperature or humidity.

Stacking boxes and containers have a long and varied history in Japanese society; originally developed as a space and labour-saving method of storing and transporting food, stacking systems have become a typical feature of contemporary design most apparent in the uniform components of technologically sophisticated music and home entertainment systems.

left: In a minimalist setting, even a television can be stored behind cupboard doors when not in use. Contemporary Japanese designers such as GK Associates use their traditional references to create complete home office workstations concealed in storage units.

above: Making the best use of available space is key to an understanding of the Zen approach to interior design. Here, the long shelves and horizontal hanging rail give a sense of order and ease of access in a small hallway.

right: Discreet and unobtrusive, an understairs cupboard provides invaluable storage space. The proportions of the doors echo the rectilinear aesthetic of this striking, minimalist interior.

left: Laid out in predetermined patterns, the module of the *tatami* mat, the standard unit of flooring in Japan, also dictates the dimensions of *fusuma*, sliding interior doors.

opposite: Seated on the *tatami* matting floor, the inhabitants can gaze out over the surrounding garden, from which they are separated by *shoji*, translucent sliding screens of paper laid over a wooden grid. The gentle transition between man-made environment and the natural world beyond is enhanced by the soft colour of the rush matting.

right: The area taken up by a single *tatami* mat defines the space needed to accommodate a sleeping adult. As a flooring surface, the *tatami* is warm and comfortable underfoot; it is also hardwearing, practical and attractive.

rectilinearity; each mat is bound along its edges with black linen or coloured brocade and then laid in a precise pattern which fills the room completely – indeed the room has been designed to accommodate the desired number of mats. The binding along the *tatami* edge not only protects the mats from fraying where two edges meet, but also gives a marked regularity and sense of order to the floor area. The pleasing visual effect of geometric repetition and the precise dimensions of the *tatami* mat are repeated in the rest of the interior. Sliding doors conform to *tatami* measurements, replicating the unit as they conceal built-in cupboards as storage for household belongings, or acting as temporary partitions between rooms. *Fusuma*, which run in

grooves between floor and lintel, function as lightweight sliding room dividers, and can be slid open or removed altogether to open up the whole floor area. Similarly, the sliding curtain walls known as *shoji* function as window and blind combined. A fine wooden grid is covered with translucent rice paper, allowing soft light into the room. The pool of sunlight thrown onto the floor is broken by rectilinear shadows thrown by the geometric structure of the screens and echoes the effect of the *tatami*.

The traditional soft mattress or *futon* naturally complies with the measurements of the *tatami* mat and is therefore in harmony with all other structural elements of the interior. The *futon* is generally the same size as a single mat, representing the sleeping

opposite: The use of standardized modular units to create a simple flexible interior originated in Japan, but has been adopted in the West to meet the needs for mass production and to create rational, harmonious, well-designed interiors.

space required by an adult. Despite their popularity in the West, double-sized *futon* are still seen as a slight oddity in Japan.

Repetition of individual units and elements to create a rhythmic whole in an otherwise uncluttered interior is strangely appealing. What is now known in modern Japan as *Yunitto-kagu* (unit furniture) has a long and honourable tradition in that culture. In the early 20th century the Dutch architect Gerrit Rietveld pioneered the development of modular systems for furniture with his spatial experiments in creating the Red/Blue Chair. The principle of mass-manufacturing components, all of which complied to certain predetermined set of dimensions, was a natural extension of industrialised manufacture, yet ironically it originated in a country where although industrialisation was new, the discipline of modular design had been known and applied for centuries. The potential for pre-fabricating standardised building parts, furniture and fittings in Modernist interiors did not escape the pragmatic designers at the Bauhaus, and architects such as Gropius and Le Corbusier were keen to create rational systems for their revolutionary new buildings, for reasons commercial as well as aesthetic. They were not the first Westerners, however, to respond to the emphasis on rectilinearity, whose crispness of effect greatly influenced the more progressive designers, perhaps because it was the complete antithesis of the ersatz opulence to be found in Victorian and Edwardian interiors. Stylistic echoes of the pillar-and-lintel construction typical of traditional Japanese architecture occur in the avant-garde interior and furniture designs of Godwin, the Greene Brothers and Eileen Gray. Frank Lloyd Wright was so enamoured of both the form and the principle of modular construction that in 1914, he designed the prestigious Imperial Hotel in Tokyo to comply with a module of his own devising, 173 centimetres (5 feet 8 inches), his own height, which he took to be the midpoint between the stature of the Japanese and western visitors.

In adopting his own height as an arbitrary module from which to create a complex and innovative structure, Wright instinctively

recognized one of the key reasons for the success of modular design – its ergonomic nature and consequent ease of use for average-sized adults.

Modularity systematizes physical actions and provides a sense of order and harmony; in the tea ceremony, the position of every utensil is decided after careful consideration of the available space. As in the *cha-shitsu* or tea house, traditional Zen-style interiors are designed to be viewed from a seated position on the floor. From this vantage point, the black borders of the *tatami* mats, the slats of the ceiling, the decorative carved lintel or *ramma* produce a visually pleasing rectilinearity which is echoed in the wooden latticework of sliding doors and windows, and in the structural crossbeams and pillars. Contemporary Zen-inspired architects continue to work within the modular idiom even if they no longer use traditional, natural materials.

The innovative architect Toyo Itoh designed his family home in Tokyo using industrial components such as aluminium sheeting and perforated steel panels. All were created in standard sizes and were, therefore, in effect, modern-day interpretations of the centuries-old principle of modularity.

Modular design is widely recognised as the ideal practical solution to the provision of economically viable mass-manufactured units, and has a great deal of visual appeal. A rectilinear format can be used to break up and articulate what would otherwise be a flat surface – from a wall of built-in storage units and shelves to the repetition of rectangular screening elements, or to subdivide shower doors in bathrooms. Conversely, free-standing screens help to articulate an open space without enclosing it; within small apartments, modular room dividers add to the sense of ordered harmony without reducing the overall impression of space. Prefabricated storage systems provide the homogeneity and unity of surface which is ideal for functional rooms such as kitchens, typically Zen ordered workplaces when well designed.

n a t u r a l
m a t e r i a l s

In the centuries-old Taoist tradition, which ultimately influenced Zen, the Five Elements of

wood, fire, earth, metal and water were perceived as the key constituents of the physical world.

above: Despite their humble origins, rice, straw, rushes and reeds are often intricately woven to create traditional household artefacts of subtlety and understated beauty.

The Japanese sense of "intense sympathy with Nature", which so intrigued Sir Rutherford Alcock, the British Ambassador to Tokyo in the 1860s, continues to inform modern interpretations of the Zen philosophy. Rooted deep in the Japanese psyche is a profound reverence for the natural world and the materials obtained from it by humans – so much so that the modern Japanese lumberjack will bow and offer his apologies to the tree he is about to fell.

Traditional Japanese architecture is predominantly a celebration of wood, used functionally to create lightweight structures of great strength and flexibility. Wooden components are rarely painted or disguised in any way; on the contrary, the natural grain and lustre of wooden timbers is carefully oiled and polished to enhance the subtle, individual texture of the material. Occasionally, wooden elements are left virtually untouched, such as the *tokobashira* or rustic vertical post defining one edge of the *tokonoma* alcove; it looks like the trunk of a tree because it alludes to the enlightenment achieved by the Buddha while resting under a tree. Wood is also chosen for its aesthetic appeal to all the senses, those of smell and touch as well as visual satisfaction. Cedar- or sandalwood-lined chests of drawers impart a delicate fragrance to clothing and deter insects, while the aroma of hot pine rising from a steaming wooden bathtub has evocative associations undreamt of by Proust. Wood is still used for everyday artefacts made in accordance with archaic designs; pine washbuckets and ladles, or simple wooden clogs to wear in the garden have a timeless appeal. Wood also finds new expression in modern design classics, such as Sori Yanagi's famous Butterfly Stool.

In a country so chronically short of natural materials, bamboo continues to have both a functional role and a symbolic significance. It is tough, lightweight, virtually waterproof and flexible, and therefore well-suited for structural use both inside and outside the home: for scaffolding, for the construction of new buildings, as intricately worked fencing, as hanging blinds to deflect the fierce midsummer sun, for the construction of giant parasols or *janome*, for temporary summer houses and folding fans. Bamboo is much used in that most high-minded of Zen pursuits, the tea ceremony. Many of the artefacts used in the ritual are made of bamboo, from the *ikebana* vase created from a single section of the plant to the hand-held tea whisk whose delicate bristles are individually cut from vertical slices into the stem of the bamboo itself. On occasions, even the structure of the tea room is made from bamboo. The bamboo plant grows very rapidly, up to a yard (0.91 metre) a night, if climatic conditions are favourable, and this image of vigour and resilience particularly appeals to the "warrior Zen" school. The legendary strength and fecundity of the material is also recalled in the *kadomatsu*, a traditional bamboo and native pine decoration to be found at the entrances of homes and businesses at New Year.

The natural materials available in Japan are used as much as possible in their unadorned state in order to reinforce the link between the human environment and the outside world. *Tatami* mats are closely-woven of rushes and give off a pleasing smell like fresh straw. Intricately-woven baskets of willow or vine are unique and expressive in shape, and much prized by modern collectors for

right: Timber, left exposed and un-adorned, reveals its uniquely rich and natural texture.

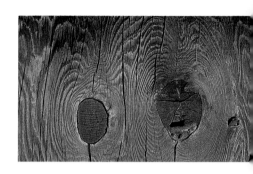

right: In the Zen spirit; daylight fills the simple, minimal-ist bathroom, emphasizing the gentle contrasts between a variety of natural materials.

full of hot water, before finally lowering oneself gingerly into the tub to relax and unwind. The other aspect of Japanese bathing that raises western eyebrows is the convivial, even communal nature of the event. The country has over one thousand natural hot springs; communal bath-houses tend to be segregated by gender, and are often a focal point in the neighbourhood, a chance to gossip with one's neighbours in chummy, if steamy, surroundings. However, bathing in a hot natural spring in the open air, surrounded by a dramatic panorama of snow-covered mountains, rocks and trees at dusk, is also a truly Zen experience.

The cleansing power of running water is a spiritual element with a great deal of symbolism to the Japanese. The country is both mountainous and volcanic, so natural springs, waterfalls, rivers and geysers are part of the natural landscape to a level largely unknown in the West. Despite a certain amount of caution of the power of the sea, owing to a well-founded fear of tidal waves, water is seen as a largely benevolent force, the medium which allows rice to grow, and is the source of new life and regeneration. Zen gardens often include ponds and trickling waterfalls, representing the outside world in miniature. Stone troughs located at the entrances to temples and shrines and great palaces offer the footsore visitor a welcome respite while he

right: In a small bathroom the integral handbasin and mirror admirably fulfil their functions and give an impression of extended space.

below: Order and clarity in the domestic interior is central to Zen; the house is designed to be easy to clean and maintain through the rigorous exclusion of clutter.

opposite: Essentially functional and serviceable, the bathroom can also be a haven and a place for aesthetic and sensual pleasure. The large window giving onto a vista of trees echoes the traditional rural Japanese bath.

left: The disciplined arrangement of space and work surfaces gives a sense of clarity and order to the modern kitchen. Not only does it look "beautiful" in the Japanese sense of being both clean and neat, it is also easy to keep spotless.

opposite: The high-tech approach to interior design is the epitome of functionality, yet in its austerity of taste and truth to materials owes a debt to the principles of Zen.

washes his hands, using a simple long-handled dipper made from sections of bamboo. Ritual cleansing before entering a holy place is associated with spiritual purity throughout the Far East; interestingly, however, the sense of "cleanliness" is not equated in Zen Buddhism with bodily asceticism and self-denial. Throughout the Far East, the lotus is the symbol of Buddhism, but in Japan the lotus is often depicted with its roots growing in mud, symbolising the gradual progress from chaos to order, from the darkness of ignorance to the flowering of enlightenment. While to a Zen devotee cleanliness is not necessarily next to godliness, for all Japanese the physical and psychological importance of cleanliness and order is a vital aid on the path towards *satori*.

above: As in the Japanese tradition, every dish or bowl has a specific function. Each receptacle for food served at a meal should be carefully selected for its appropriateness to its contents, heightening the aesthetic appeal of the feast.

below: A simple vase of delicate, balletic arum lilies softens the angles of a minimalist interior.

right: The Japanese aesthetic term *mono no aware* – "to understand the appeal of objects to the human heart" – informs the Zen-influenced interior.

opposite: Symbolic of regrowth and regeneration, living plants are an essential element in traditional Japanese homes.

In the West, we have always in the past tended to create homes which have fixed focal points: the archetypal, formal sitting room with its symmetrically-located massive chimney breast and mantelpiece is typically loaded with social signifiers, instantly recognizable symbols of status and aspiration such as ornate ornaments and invitations, and topped with a flashy painting or mirror. There is no equivalent in the Japanese household; similarly, there is generally an absence of massive pieces of furniture or ornate wall decorations. While a Zen-inspired room may have a geometric, rectilinear feel about it, such focal points as there are tend to be asymmetrically disposed. Simple, low-key interiors are deliberately kept fluid and flexible to meet the varying needs of the household and adaptable to the different activities going on within it at different times of day.

The focal point of a Zen style room is the *tokonoma* or built-in alcove, fitted with a low wooden shelf some 20 centimetres (8 inches) above the level of the *tatami*-matted floor. Set off to one side from the rest of the room, it is the recess which can be seen as the window to the soul.

The central significance of the *tokonoma* is underlined by the use of a rustic wooden vertical pillar which defines one edge of the recess. Known as the *tokobashira*, its rough, unfinished surface echoes that of a single tree trunk and makes an effective allusion to the belief that Buddha found enlightenment while sheltering under a tree. The *tokonoma* functions as a large-scale, three-dimensional frame and is an infinitely variable setting for

right: Bonsai is the centuries-old Japanese practice of cultivating landscapes in miniature to symbolize the natural world in microcosm.

personal expression. So important is it to the Zen follower that a single, well-off family may own scores of lovingly treasured flower receptacles and scroll paintings. Even the humblest household will strive to acquire a set of artefacts for each of the four seasons, and to be out of step is as ridiculous to the Japanese as it would be for Westerners to decorate and proudly display a Christmas tree in August. In the *tokonoma*, it is rare to find more than three or four objects at any one time: generally a hanging scroll, depicting an idealized landscape or a topical poem written in the free-flowing style of traditional calligraphy known as *shodo*; on the shelf is a traditional flower arrangement or *ikebana*, artfully contrived from some foliage appropriate to the season; occasionally some fruit or other natural forms, such as a piece of driftwood or weathered rock; and usually a single stick of incense, giving off a gently undulating column of fragrant smoke.

These objects are selected and arranged by the householder with all the care of a professional artist setting up a still life; the individual elements must be harmonious one with another, but they must also provoke thought and please the eye, the one attribute being dependent on the other. Any arrangement is seen as being temporary; constantly renewed and replaced according to the changing seasons or even the occasion, the *tokonoma* is both an aid to contemplation and a manifestation of the Buddhist principle of *mujo*, the impermanence of all things. Unlike western habits of installing extrovert artworks which stay in the same place year after year, eventually becoming invisible through their very familiarity, the individual aesthetic elements in the Zen interior are constantly re-evaluated, edited out and replaced when no longer apposite. The choice of natural items as an aid to contemplation can be as apparently simple as a handful of chestnut leaves and a couple of freshly-fallen conkers, radiant in colour and redolent of the onset of autumn. Such transitory, overlooked features of everyday life serve as a symbol that all aspects of this existence are fleeting, that this precise moment will never come again; they are a humbling reminder of the complexity and infinite variety of Nature. Nothing one can ever buy or create by hand can ever rival the profligate diversity of the natural world.

Ikebana is an archetypally Zen practice; it requires conscious thought to select or collect appropriate components, and the contemplation of the final result should be a further aid to meditation. Layered with symbolic meaning and intrinsically linked to the passage of seasons and the landscape around the property, *ikebana* arrangements can follow set formats but nevertheless each arrangement is unique and personal by nature of the raw materials used in its making. Similarly the practice most closely linked with Zen in the Western mind is the *sado*, usually translated as the tea ceremony but actually meaning "The Way of Tea", a semantically significant difference as the Japanese reading encompasses the whole pursuit of ritual and ceremony as an aid to contemplation. Developed into a complex and intricate art form by early Zen masters, the significance of tea-drinking is founded upon the rustic simplicity of the utensils, the consummate skill required to conduct the ceremony effectively, the formalized speech required of all participants, and the importance of following an archaic ritual surrounded by the natural world.

The relationship with the outside world is also seen by Zen devotees as crucial to fostering meditation – the communal practices of moon viewing or cherry-blossom viewing are still a part of everyday life, and Zen practitioners and poets have always revelled in the changes of the seasons, the extremes of weather, the croaking of frogs on summer evenings, the first snows or the late flowering of the last chrysanthemum. Their writings celebrate the transience of all things but also stress the profound sense of wonder to be obtained from the contemplation of Nature. It has been remarked that the Japanese tend to focus on the specific to the exclusion of the general and it is interesting that throughout the country there are many sites considered to be of great natural beauty which attract travellers from great distances. They are prepared to queue for hours to see the "perfect" view from the "ideal" vantage place, yet large tracts of countryside, to an outsider apparently equally impressive, attract little attention. It is as though certain vistas are deemed worthy of concentration, while others are not.

The same is true of the domestic interior; while it is fluid and flexible, there are key spots which are designated appropriate for contemplation and aesthetic pleasure. It is the perceived value of the shared experience which governs these slightly puzzling contradictions of where and when one can find aesthetic inspiration; while meditation is an intensely personal voyage of discovery, shared thoughts and observations, obliquely worded as all polite speech must be, may result in the "sudden" enlightenment so greatly desired by Zen practitioners.

Whether aesthetic focal points are fixed or fluid, there are useful lessons for Westerners to learn from the Zen approach. Rather like the William Morris principle, "Have nothing in your homes that you do not know to be useful or believe to be beautiful", the underlying ethos of the Zen interior is one of aesthetically pleasing functionality, an emphasis on the reduction rather than accumulation of the clutter of everyday life,

below: English Arts and Crafts designer William Morris famously stated "Have nothing in your homes that you do not know to be useful or believe to be beautiful". In the Zen tradition, even the humblest tools and artefacts of everyday life are designed to be aesthetically pleasing.

above: In a minimalist interior, *mono no aware* objects which "appeal to the human heart" have a resonance and profundity which they would lack in a more conventional setting.

opposite: The interior has been designed to highlight the favourite art and artefacts of the householders, emphasized by juxtaposition with reductionist architectural elements.

left: "Less is more" – by creating endlessly flexible interiors, we allow ourselves to focus on the specific to the exclusion of the general.

and the use of inspirational forms at key points. These could be anything visually appealing and in some way significant to the inhabitants. Matsura Katzumie succinctly describes this unorthodox approach as "resourceful eclecticism", and defines it as making the best possible use of all the available materials and resources which are appropriate to the time, the mood and one's personal circumstances. Unusual flower arrangements and eye-catching plants are thrown into sharp relief by juxtaposition with architectural elements and are a subtle reminder of the natural world.

Focal points need not be grand or impressive; instead they can be as personal as an assortment of favourite pictures, prints or photos, a carefully positioned collection of shells, sea-washed pebbles or sinuous driftwood, or a harmonious group of old

ceramics. The Modernist Japanese architect, Tadao Ando, whose innovative and radical work has been greatly influenced by Zen philosophy, advocates the creation of "a concentrated world" in the domestic interior, combining disciplined simplicity with elements which gladden the eye and may provide an intimate, personalized and therefore highly relevant aid to meditation. In a minimalist setting, these *mono no aware* objects achieve a drama and resonance they would lack in a more cluttered setting. Where possible it is desirable to experiment, to add, subtract or replace elements until satisfied with one's own contemplative still life. The Zen-style interior is a place where one can focus on the particular to the exclusion of the general, by creating endlessly variable, highly personal and infinitely expressive compositions.

below: The low shelf set into the turn in the stairs functions rather like a *tokonoma* – it can house a selection of expressive natural forms to create a personal "still life".

right: Informed by *shodo*, traditional Japanese calligraphy, this contemporary abstract artwork by Toko Shinoda has a dynamic appeal that invites contemplation.

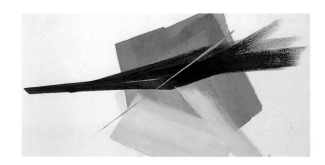

opposite: This minimalist and highly personal interior provides a variety of appealing focal points which function as a sequence of contemplative "still lives". Individually neither grand nor impressive, the components have been carefully selected to please the eye.

In recent years, Westerners have been encouraged to think of the garden as another room of the house, and to treat it accordingly.

In Japan, there is a centuries-old tradition of "blurring the boundaries" between interior and exterior, and the indigenous architecture is a physical manifestation of the perceived symbiosis between the natural and the man-made world. But within Zen, the garden is much more important than merely another room – it is a source of inspiration, a reminder of *mujo*, the transience of all things, a constantly self-renewing aid for contemplation and, in the case of formal stone gardens, a representation in miniature of the cosmos. So important is the Japanese appreciation of the natural world that modern city dwellers still participate in time-honoured social rituals, such as the autumnal moon viewing festivities, or cherry-blossom viewing picnics in spring. Graphic symbols derived from the transition of the seasons are instantly recognizable to most Japanese and proliferate in advertising and all forms of cultural phenomena. Plum or cherry blossom signifies spring; willow stands for summer; gingko leaves or chrysanthemums are associated with autumn, while the New Year is marked by bamboo and native pine. Similarly, *kimono* are decorated with seasonal plant motifs, and playing cards are decorated with the representative motifs of each of the four seasons, rather than each of the four suits common in the West. It is as though the people of this recently industrialized country still hanker for the visual signals of the impermanence and constant mutability of the natural world.

The concept of privacy is one which is consciously cultivated in even the tiniest domestic garden in Japan, where solitude is both a status symbol and an aid to meditation. The boundaries are enclosed by rough-hewn stone walls or closely-bound bamboo fencing. Plants are deliberately cultivated to grow up around the building and the plot limits. By using large-leafed bushes close to the house and small-leafed ones or even miniature trees such as acer on the outer extremities, Japanese garden designers create an interesting trompe l'oeil effect, of the landscape apparently stretching away into infinity. The apparent sense of randomness and naturalness is in fact carefully cultivated, and generally includes a number of key elements perceived to be essential – meandering footpaths, interestingly-shaped weathered rocks, plants and bushes with symbolic connotations which provide all-year round interest, a water feature of some sort, whether a gently trickling fountain, a pond containing koi carp, or a rustic stone trough with a bamboo dipper. The garden has been deliberately designed to provide a sequence of viewpoints which function as an aid to contemplation.

The strategies which inform and shape so much of Japanese architecture have been successfully applied by progressive western designers. The tradition of sliding walls which vanish to open the house into the garden have found new expression throughout Europe, Australasia and America. Raised verandas sheltered by overhanging eaves offer the ideal spot from which to view the garden, and wooden decking extends from the veranda into the garden itself.

Inside the house architects and designers are making increasing use of the shifting angles and different intensities of sunlight to create constantly changing environments. Bringing natural forms into the house further strengthens the link between external and internal. Living plants, evocative flower arrangements or assemblies of natural forms worn by the passage of time act as focal points in

opposite: In a tiny, enclosed courtyard in a traditional inn in Kyoto, a stone water trough and bamboo hint at the natural world beyond the man-made environment.

left: Sliding glass doors barely separate the garden from the interior, blurring the boundaries between the inside and the outside.

left: Overhanging eaves protect the inhabitants from sun while the low-level windows and veranda seem to bring the garden into the bedroom.

opposite: A covered walkway allows the inhabitants to appreciate the inner courtyard garden even when the weather is too cold or wet to open the sliding glass doors.

an otherwise minimalist setting, softening the rigorous simplicity of a largely rectilinear scheme.

The Zen attitude to the external world is a key to understanding the nature of the philosophy itself, and is revealed in the respect shown to all living beings. Intimately bound up with the search for personal enlightenment, the individual sees himself as both dependent on the natural world and at the same time a potentially benign factor in its development and protection. "Gardening" in the Zen sense means collecting the fallen leaves and twigs to burn in a brazier, giving heat to the interior; it might involve carefully raking the gravel into intricate patterns evocative of stylized waves. However it does not generally include "gardening" in the western sense, the unceremonious eviction of lichens and mosses, or the "scorched earth" policy of applying weedkiller to unwanted plants. This attitude was exemplified in the life of the Zen poet and hermit, Ryokan, who was concerned to discover some fast-growing bamboo shoots which had taken root and were sprouting at an alarming rate beneath the floorboards of his raised wooden veranda. He cut a hole in the beams to allow the bamboo to flourish – a very Zen solution.

left: Interior and exterior blur in the traditional teahouse and stone garden.
Interestingly, the whole complex is actually set inside a modern building in Manhattan and is used for teaching of *Cha no yu*, "The Way of Tea", the archetypal Zen experience.

right: The contemplation of the infinitely variable seasons and the mutability of the natural world allow the devotee to appreciate the essence of *mushin* or the transience of human existence, and is crucial to an understanding of Zen Buddhism.

left: The wooden veranda provides a raised viewpoint looking out over the garden; the meandering stone path appears to lead into the distance and it becomes impossible to discern the boundaries of the plot.

gardens

"The grasses of the garden

They fall,

And lie as they fall."

RYOKAN (c. 1758-1831)

Visiting a Zen temple in Kyoto, you sit quietly on the *tatami*, gazing out into the light of the garden. The expanse of white gravel before you is an empty vessel into which you can pour your deepest thoughts. It beckons the spirit and the spirit follows.

Drawn out of yourself, you slip into a different plane of consciousness and time slips by unnoticed. When it comes time to leave, you do so refreshed as if you had been taking in the salt air along a rocky seashore or climbing through mist-shrouded valleys in the depths of the mountains. The garden has the capacity to change your focus, to release from within you new thoughts and new perceptions – of beauty, of life, of the meaning of existence. What is this mystical power and from where does it issue? How can we capture it, or even a fragment of it, for our own life and garden? To understand this, we must reflect on the origins of these extraordinary gardens.

setting the scene

Zen Buddhism first came to Japan from China in the early years of the Japanese imperial court (*see also pages 7-11*), but it found little fertile soil to grow in at that time. Society was governed by an aristocratic class which seemed to prefer the complexity and pomp of the esoteric sects of Buddhism: austere Zen withered. Several hundred years later, the military class replaced the aristocratic class in Japan as the power base of society. The new leaders moved their capital to Kamakura, an isolated town near present-day Tokyo, giving name to the era, the Kamakura period (1185-1333). Zen Buddhism was reintroduced from China at this time and flourished under the support of the *shogun* (chief military lord) and *daimyo* (vassal lords). Some of the basic tenets of Zen Buddhism (e.g. the emphasis on rigorous self-training as a

means to enlightenment and a freedom from attachments to worldly things), were accepted easily by the military class who readily adapted them to their own way of life. Also, the new Zen sects did not have a power base, nor were they landed like the old Japanese Buddhist sects which made Zen priests less likely to be politically meddlesome. Most importantly, Zen Buddhism was new, it was the wave of the future, and the new military leaders and the priests of the new religion fell in line together.

Yet the gardens of the Kamakura period did not look like what is now referred to as a Zen garden. Rather, from what we can construe of them through remnant gardens, images in medieval paintings or archeological digs, they seem to be merely extensions of the aristocratic gardens from an earlier time. Then a change occurred which was to have a massive effect on society, setting the course for Zen Buddhism as a religion and more so, for Zen Buddhism as the primary influence on the arts of Japan, including the garden – the military lords moved their capital back to Kyoto. Leaving Kamakura, the *shogun* now took up residence in the ancient capital where the emperor and his aristocratic court continued to live. Though he had lost his power to rule the nation in the distant past, the emperor continued to reign as the spiritual leader of Japan and also, with his retinue of genteel aristocrats, as the protector and purveyor of high culture.

The *shogun's* choice for government headquarters in Kyoto was the central Muromachi district, which gave its name to the Muromachi period (1333-1568) during which Kyoto developed into a prosperous merchant town. In Kyoto one could find the finest materials for effecting a cultured life – silk and cotton

left: Zen temples of the Muromachi period were centres of artistic exchange as well as of religious training. Many of the gardens which stem from that time were inspired by images of mountains lost in layers of mist. They remind us of those in the ink landscape paintings of Sung-dynasty China which were the height of fashion at that time.

cloth, refined pottery and laquerware, paper and food stuffs –
and it was the merchant class that had the financial capability
and expertise to produce and distribute these goods. Thus in
Kyoto during the Muromachi period there was a confluence of
three classes of society, mixing in a manner that had never been
seen before in Japan. This triumvirate included powerful military
lords who set the masculine tone of the era, controlling the
workings of society (for better or worse) with their well-honed
swords; wealthy merchants who were the purveyors of refined
materials that supported high culture; and learned Zen priests
who introduced a religion and philosophy that gave deeper
meaning to the actions of the time. All this rested on the mantle
of the imperial court, which lent respectability and legitimacy to
society while invoking its cultural air.

the birth of the garden

The scene was now set for the flowering of what we now call
the Zen arts – Noh theatre, tea, flower arranging, architecture,
and gardens. The biggest influence on the arts of the day was
the culture of Sung-dynasty China, especially the minimalistic
black and white ink landscapes which had been popular in Japan
since the Kamakura period. Now, in China, the Mongols had
invaded from the north and the Sung dynasty was moribund.
Chinese priests invited to reside in Japan were only too happy to
find a means to flee their troubled country and when they left,
they brought with them many cultural artefacts from their
homeland. In this way, the Zen temples of Kyoto came to be
home to many Chinese priests as well as large collections of
Chinese artwork. Throughout the Muromachi period, these collections were greatly increased by the introduction of new
artworks purchased by trade missions sent to China as part of
what is known as "the tally trade". The influence of these

opposite: The
main hall of Zen
temples, called a
hojo, was entered
through a roofed
gate that opened
onto an empty
court. At some
point, artists
began using
these courts for
the creation of
gardens which
were imbued
with the austere
aesthetics of
the time.

left: The Hiden-
in, Kyoto. The
path is the central
element of the tea
garden (which is
properly called a
roji). Evoking the
sensory qualities
of a walk into the
deep mountains,
the *roji* guides
guests to the
teahouse while
also symbolizing
progression to a
deeper state of
consciousness.

opposite: The stroll gardens of the Edo period were based on the aesthetics of the tea garden although much more complex and grander in scale. Many of the elements that were first used in gardens by the early teamasters, such as lanterns, also became essential parts of stroll gardens.

artworks, especially the ink landscapes called *sansui-ga*, or "mountain water paintings", was central to shaping the gardens we find in Zen temples.

Zen temples of the Muromachi period were based on a form of Chinese architecture that, over a period of centuries, had been tailored to suit the physical environment of Japan and cultural taste of the Japanese people. One common feature of all the temples was a main hall called a *hojo* (which means 3 metres/ 10 feet square), suggesting a simplicity and paucity which were held to be ideals of the time, even though these halls were actually much larger than their name implies. To the south of the main hall was an open court that was used as a formal entry to the building. In time, however, the use of this space as an entry was superseded by the development of the *genkan*, a formal entry connected to an annex allowing access to the *hojo* without crossing the southern courtyards which, in turn, fell out of use.

At some point, Zen priests began experimenting with creating gardens in the empty courts using the imagery from the Sung-dynasty ink landscape paintings as motifs for their garden design. The steeply rising layers of mountains found in the paintings assumed physical form in the gardens as rocks thrusting up from the ground plane. The untouched expanses of paper which in the paintings had evoked the image of hovering clouds or mist or the spreading surface of the sea, were now interpreted in the gardens by spreading the ground with a layer of fine white gravel.

Such minimalistic expressions of landscapes made with rock, sand and sometimes a few carefully placed evergreen plants, are

properly called *kare-san-sui* or "dry mountain water". This term partially reflects the fact that these gardens were expressions of mountains and water (the sea or at times a river), as in the ink paintings, and also conveys the sense that as they were made without any actual water they could be said to be "dry". Also, since ancient times in Japan the expression "mountain-water" (*san-sui* or *senzui*, as it was pronounced in earlier times), meant "garden". In this light we see that the expression *kare-san-sui*, simply meaning "dry garden", implies that this is just a gardening style (unconnected with whether it represents mountains and water or not) which does not use water.

The first way to perceive the gardens in Zen temples, therefore, is as an artwork inspired by the most influential artwork of the era, ink landscape paintings which were Chinese in origin though not necessarily related to Chinese *Ch'an* Buddhist sects (*Ch'an* being the Chinese pronunciation of Zen). Rather, they can be said to be part and parcel of the larger world of the Chinese literati which included, but was not limited to, *Ch'an* Buddhist concepts. The aesthetics of the paintings are very similar to those found in the design of the garden. For instance the unpainted areas of the ink paintings and the wide expanses of sand in the gardens are both described with the word *ma*, meaning a void in space or time. With both the gardens and the paintings, this emptiness allows the viewer mentally to "enter" and explore his or her own perceptions which a more "complete" work would not allow.

above: Before entering the tea house, guests rinse their mouth and hands at a water laver, *tsukubai*, in a ritual act of spiritual cleansing. The gentle sound of falling water can be introduced to the garden here but during a tea gathering the running water will be turned off. At that time the laver holds the same water that will be used to make tea.

meditation
gardens

In the West, dry gardens are often known as meditation gardens, which is extremely misleading. The image created by the term is that dry gardens are used as the focal point of daily seated meditation; this is simply not true. In monastic life, priests most commonly meditate in *zen-do*, darkened halls that cut off extraneous influences that would disturb meditation.

In fact, priests may meditate wherever they feel the mood and there are times, like *yaza* or night-time sitting, during which they sit before the garden, but it never becomes the actual focus of meditation.

There are at least two ways, however, in which Zen Buddhism and the gardens are related. First, according to Zen thought, there are two "methods" of meditating, the stillness or seated method, and the moving method. The moving method refers to all daily chores or movements: cleaning temple halls, tending vegetable patches, sweeping fallen leaves, as well as raking gravel in gardens; all are forms of moving meditation. In this way the daily care of the garden is an integral part of temple life and a means of meditation. Nowadays, both in Japan and in the West, dry gardens are desired because they are perceived to be low-maintenance whereas, in fact, care of the garden is one of the most fundamental reasons for its existence.

The second connection between Zen thought and the gardens can be seen in the way some Buddhist concepts can be perceived in the design of the gardens as allegorical messages expressed through an austere palette of rocks and sand. Two such concepts are *ku* (emptiness or non-substantiality) and *shinnyo* (suchness or thusness). *Ku*, a fundamental concept of all Buddhist sects, embodies the idea that the world is "empty" or, more accurately, that it is empty of inherent existence. What better way to express this concept of emptiness than a void, an expanse of white sand? Moreover, since the sand is representative of water, as an ocean or as a river, it also aptly expresses impermanence, another manifestation of *ku*. Related to this is the concept of *shinnyo*, a term that means the true nature of things, a reality "as-it-is". Here again, what better way to get across this blunt yet ethereal concept than to just to sit and look at a rock? The rock is. How simple, how direct!

below: The southern garden of Daisen-in temple, Kyoto, contains an image of the broad ocean, or perhaps of emptiness. The single tree in the south west corner, *Ficus religiosa*, is reminiscent of the one under which the Buddha meditated and realized his enlightenment. A double-layered hedge rather than the traditional earth wall encloses the garden.

right: The austere palette of rocks and sand aptly captures the essence of the Buddhist concepts of suchness and emptiness.

The layering of stones in dry gardens creates a sense of depth, accentuated here by the use of flat stones which are placed tightly against one another. The inclusion of a small pool of water brings an element of the tea garden into this *kare-san-sui* or "dry mountain water" garden created for its North American owners.

tea gardens

By the end of the Muromachi period (1568), Zen Buddhism had become well established in Kyoto, as had the relationship between the triumvirate of *daimyo*, merchants and priests.

Collecting Chinese artworks became the main pastime of the wealthy, and parties were thrown with the intent of drinking tea and displaying one's finery – porcelain tea-bowls, bronze flower vases, and ink landscape paintings by famous Chinese or Japanese artists. The tone of these gatherings was ostentatious, and in reaction to this over-emphasis on the trappings of wealth, certain connoisseurs of culture – Zen priests as well as merchants – proposed a new vision of a tea gathering. The taking of tea, they suggested, should not be held in the formal hall but rather in a rustic, thatched hut, where simple, rough crockery, as might be used by farmers, would take the place of the grand porcelain and bronze of China. The flowers displayed should be simple, few in number and should appear as if they had just been picked and set casually in the vase. In all, the tone of the tea gatherings they proposed was one of reserve and understated elegance, an aesthetic that these tea masters called *wabi*.

To prepare for and attain the appropriate mental repose for a *wabi* tea gathering, an entry way was now required, and this was the impetus for creating the tea garden or *roji*, as it is properly called. Even as the *soan* teahouse was reminiscent of a hermit's hut in the faraway mountains, so the *roji* became a reflection of a path to that hut. The *roji*, which translates as "dewy path", took all of the sensory experience of leaving town and climbing up into an ever-deepening forest along a narrow path and compressed it into the confined space of an urban Zen temple, or a *daimyo* or merchant residence.

The tea gardens of today have certain requisite components that stem from this period:

First is the outer gate which, once entered, closed and locked, separates the guests from the outer world. Next, the guests move forward to a roofed waiting bench, *koshikake machiai*, where they are allowed time to rest, adjust their clothes, if necessary, and commune with the ephemeral sensations of Nature in the garden. Called forward by their host, the guests will then pass through a middle gate which symbolizes the passage into a state of deeper awareness. As the entry to the tea house draws near, the guests will find a *chiri-ana*, or dust-pit – in effect a small tile-lined hole into which garden debris can be temporarily swept. At the time of a tea gathering, the *chiri-ana* holds one evergreen bow and a pair of bamboo debris-pickers which symbolize the preparations that the host has made. Finally, the guests enter the teahouse through a small square opening (*nijiri-guchi*). Once the teahouse is entered, the *nijiri-guchi* is closed, and the garden disappears from view, not to be seen during the tea gathering. Its only function is to act as an entryway – a spiritual passage from the profane world into the rarefied world of tea.

Some of the early tea masters were Zen priests, others were merchants or *daimyo* connected to the artistic world of the large Zen temples in Kyoto. In this way, Zen Buddhism became a backdrop, or foundation, for the development of tea and many of the fundamental concepts that are found in Zen Buddhism are also revealed in a tea gathering.

opposite: Cut-leafed maples are not used commonly in gardens in Japan although they have become widely used as elements representative of Japanese gardens in the West, as here in a Seattle garden. Especially favoured are weeping varieties that remain red throughout the year. These trees have a naturally dwarfed growth pattern which reduces the need for a trained gardener in order to produce a sculptural result.

left: The reuse of old architectural stone in a new way was first experimented with by the early teamasters. Here, at Kyoto's Ryoan-ji temple, an old foundation stone has been given new life in the garden as a water laver.

In the past, garden materials were drawn from Nature, with a small admixture of man-made elements for accent. The use of cut granite in the garden, as is becoming more prevalent these days, is partly in response to availability and partly as a result of a new aesthetic which appreciates these manufactured forms. This water feature was created by a Japanese designer for an English garden.

opposite: Siting structures such as a gazebo or pavilion properly is imperative to its success. Key factors are the way in which it will be incorporated as part of the entire composition of the garden and, conversely, how the garden itself will be revealed from the vantage point of the building.

above: Looking into the Ryoan-ji temple garden, Kyoto. From this position all the the sounds and scents of the area can be appreciated, as well as the garden itself.

s t r o l l   g a r d e n s

As Japan progressed through the Edo period (1600-1868), the country stabilized politically and economically, allowing for the establishment of large estates.

The owners of these properties were either the powerful provincial lords or, in some cases, aristocrats who still remained in Kyoto. The salient feature of the estates was their size. Passed from generation to generation, the gardens grew progressively, incorporating surrounding land as they enlarged. While the basis for the design of these gardens was the tea *roji* and an act of compression, the gardens of large Edo-period estates were designed through expansion, as revealed in their common name, stroll gardens. Whereas no one in Japan would call these gardens "zen gardens", their derivation from the tea *roji* in some way links them back to the foundation of Zen thought.

Many of the characteristic features of the stroll gardens – for instance, stepping stones and stone lanterns – were first used in gardens by the early tea masters, while some of the design techniques employed were altogether new.

Most stroll gardens incorporate a series of scenes linked together by a path that alternately reveals and conceals them through a technique called hide and reveal (*mie-kagure*). In some gardens, the scenes were reminiscent of famous places in Japan such as Mount Fuji or Ama-no-hashidate, the Bridge to Heaven on the Inland Sea, north of Kyoto. Others were drawn from visions of China, although none of the garden designers actually went to China to see first-hand, for instance, West Lake or Mount Lu, a place of Buddhist pilgrimage. Still others were drawn from poetry or fantasies of country life in which the lords wished to participate but, for social reasons, could not. The scenes were usually not recreated in the garden *in toto*, as if building a model, but rather were expressed by the inclusion of some rarefied element which would symbolize them. The peninsula Ama-no-hashidate, for example, was devised in Katsura Rikyu, the garden of an aristocratic prince, simply by building a spit of land out into the pond and planting it with one elegant pine tree. This simple technique of recreation by association can be used today by gardeners in any culture in the design of gardens.

opposite: Many plants within Japanese gardens contain allegorical meaning. Some pines for instance are termed either female (*mem-matsu*) or male (*on-matsu*). The soft needles and general lightness of the red pine have given it its feminine image, while the stiffer angular forms of the black pine have caused it to be associated with masculine imagery.

left: Bridges, such as this one at Kenroku-en, in Kanazawa, hold deep significance in Japanese gardens. Not only do they allow water to be crossed, they imply the passage from one world to another; usually from our own, profane world through to another, more enlightened one.

above: The juxtaposition of beauty created by the human hand with the beauty of Nature is the fundamental aesthetic of Japanese gardens. This concept is expressed elegantly in this garden in New England by the way the crisp slate steps, clearly man-made, have been sensitively fitted into the natural convolutions of the existing ledge.

above: Stone lanterns are used nowadays almost exclusively for their sculptural qualities as here, in the gardens of the International Hotel, Kyoto. In traditional tea gardens, however, before the invention of electric lighting, they were very much used as lights and the number of wicks placed in the oil lamp (for brightness) was determined by the varying strength of the moonlight.

opposite: Huntington Botanical Gardens, Los Angeles area. A rocky shore, *ara-iso* in Japanese, has been a garden motif since ancient times in Japan and is even mentioned as a garden style in the 11th-century gardening text, *Sakutei-ki*. The image is symbolic of an ocean bay where strong winds and waves have exposed the boulders on the beach.

right: The eye is drawn to a weathered tree, nearly dead, which has been included in the garden. The succession of life and death, a primal truth of the human condition, is not something to be excluded from the garden.

above: The design of this New England garden merges the geometry of the architecture with the organic mounding of the distant trees through the middle ground formed by the patio. Although composed of rectilinear pavers, the man-made patio pays homage to Nature where it abuts stones and plantings.

elements of design

In trying to create a garden in the spirit of Zen Buddhism, it is best not only to mimic traditional forms but also to strive to incorporate the essence of the garden. The following pages present fundamental aspects of the gardens we have just looked at – palette, enclosure, space, balance, Nature and Man, the path, and garden care – as a basis for design ideas.

palette

The range of materials used in the garden must be reduced to the simplest possible. Even as Zen Buddhism seeks to achieve an understanding of the true nature of reality by stripping away the veil of false form, the garden must express itself in its simplest terms. White sand and rocks are the perfect medium for this expression. But while white sand is a locally available material in Kyoto, for designers in foreign countries, the challenge is to find a simple material in the natural world close at hand that will work as a substitute. It should be of such a nature that it will weather well with age. Simply hewn granite pavers, for instance, after they have been watered down and walked on for a period of time, take on a lustre that is impossible to create artificially.

The tendency with plants is to use a foundation of evergreens whose function is to create the form and space of the garden. Within this framework, a few deciduous or flowering plants may be added for contrast. Evergreens speak of permanence, while the impermanence of deciduous leaves and brief blooms alludes to the evanescent quality of Nature.

right: Soil is one of the basic materials of the traditional garden design palette. The striated colour bands in this rammed earth wall derive from the construction technique itself – layers of soil gradually built up upon each other inside a mould. The different colours simply reflect the variety of soils used.

left: Reduced to an austere palette of stone and sand, the garden takes on the sensory qualities of a black and white ink painting. The monochrome palette places emphasis on form rather than display of colour.

e n c l o s u r e

The further a design is reduced to its basic components, the more important the tenuous balance between those components becomes. If a garden is juxtaposed with a complex backdrop, it will lose its integrity. Just as simple ink painting or flowing calligraphy are given a frame of fabric in a hanging scroll, the Zen garden must be framed by an earthen or stone wall, by a fence of wood or bamboo or by a tightly trimmed evergreen hedge.

Such an enclosure or frame can also created by architecture, as happens when the walls of a nearby building (or buildings) form part of the enclosure surrounding the garden. Perhaps more important is the way in which the view of a garden can be revealed through the opening of a window or, as in the case of Japanese architecture, a completely open wall. The best seat to view the garden from in a Japanese home or temple is not, in fact, on the veranda but rather it is far back inside the room near the wall facing the garden. The garden then appears framed within the rectilinear opening of the building which, in combination with the wall to the rear of the garden, completes the enclosure of the garden.

opposite: At the Ryoan-ji in Kyoto the complex relationship between the forms of the stones, and the spaces that surround them, would completely break down if the garden was visually merged with the forest beyond. The earthen wall allows the garden to read as a distinct work of art, aesthetically connected to and yet physically separate from its natural surroundings.

above: The frame of the windows in the foreground divides the garden into discreet units like the panels of a folding screen. They also syncopate with the wall panels at the rear of the garden – verticals in play against a basically horizontal garden.

Japanese garden design avoids symmetry and central, axial relationships. There is no one point in the garden that is predominant, although there may be many that draw the eye – a stone lantern, a grouping of rocks, a tree with a sculptural shape. To achieve stability as well as dynamism in Japanese gardens, preference is given to the triangle as the basis for design. As any civil engineer knows – or an expert in the martial arts, for that matter – triangles are the basis for the strength of things as diverse as bridge trusses and body stances in karate. Yet, quite unlike its sedentary rectangular cousin, the triangle also offers visual dynamism.

Rock groupings in Zen gardens are almost always triangular. This does not mean there are only three stones, but rather that the outline of the overall shape, as viewed either in plan view or in elevation, forms a triangle. This is as true of one individual stone as it is a grouping of several stones. The triangular shape is not limited to rocks, but can also be found in the overall shape of trimmed plants. Pine trees, for example, spread outward from top to bottom in a pyramidal way. The triangle, however, is never recreated in the garden as a pure and exact geometric shape but is instead presented in a somewhat blurred or softened form.

above: Plantings, stones, and ornaments are placed within the garden the way an artist would dab paint on a canvas. Chosen for their colour, texture and form, the various elements of the composition play against each other.

opposite: There is no one element in the garden that dominates all others. As the rocks around the spring in this private garden in Kyoto depict, the careful choice of colours, forms, and rock placement creates an arrangement that is both stable as well as visually dynamic the way rocks in a natural stream bed would be.

There are elements of the Japanese garden which reflect aspects of wild Nature and there are those that clearly show the human hand. Neither dominates the other, rather, they exist in the garden in a harmonic balance which underpins its natural beauty. Neat walls and fences that enclose the garden, roof tiles used as borders to a gutter where rain drops from the eaves, a path made of cut granite pavers, a water basin carved into a boulder, a bridge crossing a stream – all these are manifestations of human control. Alongside them there may be many elements apparently in their natural state – rocks and stones taken from mountains or rivers, trees pruned to evoke a windswept shape, random tufts of grass bamboo or a small brook, meandering casually.

These opposing yet harmonic elements are deliberately juxta-posed so that they play against each other. Looking back across a traditional garden from a temple hall, one might see first the crisp shape of a drip-line (Man), then a planting of softly mounding moss and the organic forms of rocks (Nature) behind which lies a precise horizontal band formed by an earthen wall (Man), then some trees peeping over from the garden beyond (Nature), the roof of the neighbouring temple (Man), and finally, the sky. This interplay of man-made and natural elements becomes the basic theme of both the overall design of the garden and of the elementary details within it.

left: Some of the materials used in this Kyoto garden are drawn directly from Nature – moss, white granite gravel, red mountain soil, smooth black river pebbles. Others are man-made, such as the roof tiles that have been turned on end to edge a trench which catches rain dripping off the roof. The interplay between the organic simplicity of the former and precision of the latter is a dominant theme of this garden.

below: Both natural elements and some created by Man are woven into this garden at the Ryogen-in, Kyoto, in overlapping layers. Furthermore, the elements themselves contain aspects of both. The wall, for instance, is clearly man-made and yet it is constructed of the most basic natural material – plain earth. Moss is a natural material and yet here has taken on a circular form – evidence again of the human hand at work.

the path

In a Japanese garden, the path is more than just a route that leads from here to there. It sets the rhythm and cadence of how the garden will be experienced. Walking along a smooth path of packed earth or fine gravel, we travel with a gliding motion; feet make quick, sharp sounds when striking the ground, and, head held high, we are free to look around. In contrast, when we reach a section of small stepping stones, our motion slows, we move hesitantly from one stone to the next, our feet make muffled, quiet sounds and, having dropped our heads to give attention to our footing, the view of the surrounding garden closes in. It is possible, therefore, to affect the way in which a garden will be perceived by the design of what is placed under the visitor's feet.

The path is also suggestive of a way to a new understanding, as with the tea *roji*, which takes the guest through a spiritual change. In fact, paths built in contemplation gardens of Zen temples which are not meant to be entered at all are there specifically to suggest this. Leading from the temple hall up into the rock work in the distance, in such places the path is symbolic of a journey away from the world of Man, with its social and economic trappings, into the depths of wild Nature, called *shinzan yukoku* (deep mountains, mysterious valleys), where meditation will reveal deeper truths.

opposite: In traditional tea gardens, the path is all-important. Walking the path is part of the process of spiritual preparation required before entering the teahouse. Here, in this western garden, it leads us away from the house and down to a roofed waiting bench, *koshikake machiai*, at the rear of the garden, and then on to a tea house.

above: The long and narrow path to the Koto-in temple in Kyoto leads back through a canopy of overhanging trees. Filtered light and cool breezes wafting up from the moss evoke a transformation within visitors, so that upon arrival at the front gate they feel as if they are entering another world.

photography credits

Front cover: House & Garden/Conde Nast Publications

AA Photo Library 10bl, 13t, 13b; Annely Juda Fine Art, London 78tr; Richard Davies 21r, 23, 26, 30l, 30-31, 36t, 36b, 40, 42, 46, 47t, 47b, 51, 57, 59b, 60r, 65b, 66, 79, 81, 82-83; De La Espada 72tr; Michael Freeman 18, 41, 48, 54t, 55, 59tr, 64, 67r, 80, 84-85; Futon Company 24r, 25; Habitat, UK 52; Harpur Garden Library 89, 91, 95t, 95b, 99, 103, 112, 116, 119, 123; designer: Terry Welch, Seattle: 86, 96-97, 98; Michael Harvey 38, 43 (artist: Edmund de Waal); Marc Peter Keane 90, 110, 114, 117, 118; Lam Watson Woods 53; A S Laundon 106l, 108l, 108-109, 113, 120, 122 (design: Zen Associates); Ray Main 72bl; Jean de Meulder 61, 69; Japan National Tourist Office 6, 9cr, 9b, 10tr, 105; Clive Nichols 1, 92, 107, 111, 100-101 (designer: Hiroshi Nanamori, Chelsea 1996), 102 (designers: J Dowle and K Ninomiya, Chelsea 1995); John Pawson Architect 20, 21l, 29r, 34, 50l, 54b, 62-63, 70; David Scott 9tl, 15t, 15b, 16, 121; David Spero 22, 37, 44-45, 65tr (architect: Seth Stein); Pamla Toler 71, 85c, 85br, 87, 93, 104, 106r; EWA/Andreas von Einsiedel 32, 33l, 33r, 35, 50r, 67bc, 68tl, 68br, 77; EWA/Rodney Hyett 26, 28-29, 49, 62l, 76tl, 76main; EWA/Tom Leighton 63tr; EWA/Di Lewis 73, 78main; EWA/Tim Street-Porter 24l, 60l, 82tl

Special photography: Mark Tupper 19 (bowl and chopsticks from Habitat, UK) 74, 75

acknowledgements

David Scott would like to thank Yvonne McFarlane, Publishing Director, for having the idea for this book and the vision to see it through to realization. Anke Ueberberg for her friendly and efficient liaison work between myself and the book's production team. Siân Evans and Marc Peter Keane; the quality of their fascinating and informative contributions made my job a pleasure. Japan Airlines and Japan National Tourist Organisation for their travel and research assistance. Lucy Dossor for her computer processing skills and patience with my many text changes. Finally, an important thank you to Genpo Merzel Roshi, Abbot Kanzeon Sangha, for his long term Zen guidance and commitment to the dharma.

Siân Evans would like to thank Susannah and Roger Handley, Peter Hill and Angela Hyde-Courtney, Sarah Evans, David Kitt, Dr. Ignacio Romero, Simon Halewood, Gregory Hopewell and Clare Gogerty.

Zen Associates

The Publishers would especially like to thank Peter White and Elaine Grant of Zen Associates Inc., for lending us transparencies of their work and for their generous advice. Zen Associates Inc. is an environmental design firm providing comprehensive landscape design, landscape planning and landscape contruction services throughout the United States and abroad. Founded in 1980 by Shinichiro Abe, they have completed a wide variety of projects ranging from courtyard gardens and interior atriums to large scale site design.

Zen Associates Inc. can be contacted at:

124 Boston Post Road, Sudbury
MA 01776-24006, USA
Tel: (978) 443 6222
Toll-free (800) 834 6654
Fax: (978) 443 0368
webmaster@zenassociates.com